GERNIKA

Genealogy of a Lie

The Cañada Blanch / Sussex Academic Studies on Contemporary Spain

General Editor: Professor Paul Preston, London School of Economics

A list of all published titles in the series is available on the Press website. More recently published works are presented below.

Peter Anderson, *Friend or Foe?: Occupation, Collaboration and Selective Violence in the Spanish Civil War.*

Germà Bel, *Disdain, Distrust, and Dissolution: The Surge of Support for Independence in Catalonia.*

Carl-Henrik Bjerström, *Josep Renau and the Politics of Culture in Republican Spain, 1931–1939: Re-imagining the Nation.*

Darryl Burrowes, *Historians at War: Cold War Influences on Anglo-American Representations of the Spanish Civil War.*

Andrew Canessa (ed.), *Barrier and Bridge: Spanish and Gibraltarian Perspectives on Their Border.*

Kathryn Crameri, *'Goodbye, Spain?': The Question of Independence for Catalonia.*

Pol Dalmau, *Press, Politics and National Identities in Catalonia: The Transformation of La Vanguardia, 1881–1931.*

Mark Derby, *Petals and Bullets: Dorothy Morris – A New Zealand Nurse in the Spanish Civil War.*

Francisco Espinosa-Maestre, *Shoot the Messenger?: Spanish Democracy and the Crimes of Francoism – From the Pact of Silence to the Trial of Baltasar Garzón.*

María Jesús González, *Raymond Carr: The Curiosity of the Fox.*

Helen Graham, *The War and its Shadow: Spain's Civil War in Europe's Long Twentieth Century.*

Xabier A. Irujo, *GERNIKA: Genealogy of a Lie.*

Mandie Iveson, *Language Attitudes, National Identity and Migration in Catalonia: 'What the Women Have to Say'*

Angela Jackson, *'For us it was Heaven': The Passion, Grief and Fortitude of Patience Darton – From the Spanish Civil War to Mao's China.*

Gabriel Jackson, *Juan Negrín: Physiologist, Socialist, and Spanish Republican War Leader.*

Nathan Jones, *The Adoption of a Pro-US Foreign Policy by Spain and the United Kingdom: José María Aznar and Tony Blair's Personal Motivations and their Global Impact.*

Xavier Moreno Juliá, *The Blue Division: Spanish Blood in Russia, 1941–1945.*

David Lethbridge, *Norman Bethune in Spain: Commitment, Crisis, and Conspiracy.*

Antonio Miguez Macho, *The Genocidal Genealogy of Francoism: Violence, Memory and Impunity.*

Carles Manera, *The Great Recession: A Subversive View.*

Nicholas Manganas, *Las dos Españas: Terror and Crisis in Contemporary Spain.*

Jorge Marco, *Guerrilleros and Neighbours in Arms: Identities and Cultures of Antifascist Resistance in Spain.*

Emily Mason, *Democracy, Deeds and Dilemmas: Support for the Spanish Republic within British Civil Society, 1936–1939.*

Soledad Fox Maura, *Jorge Semprún: The Spaniard who Survived the Nazis and Conquered Paris.*

Martin Minchom, *Spain's Martyred Cities: From the Battle of Madrid to Picasso's* Guernica.

Olivia Muñoz-Rojas, *Ashes and Granite: Destruction and Reconstruction in the Spanish Civil War and Its Aftermath.*

Linda Palfreeman, *Spain Bleeds: The Development of Battlefield Blood Transfusion during the Civil War.*

Fernando Puell de la Villa and David García Hernán (eds.), *War and Population Displacement: Lessons of History.*

Rúben Serém, *Conspiracy, Coup d'état and Civil War in Seville, 1936–1939: History and Myth in Francoist Spain.*

Gareth Stockey, *Gibraltar: "A Dagger in the Spine of Spain?"*

Maggie Torres, *Anarchism and Political Change in Spain: Schism, Polarisation and Reconstruction of the* Confederación Nacional del Trabajo, *1939–1979.*

Dacia Viejo-Rose, *Reconstructing Spain: Cultural Heritage and Memory after Civil War.*

Antoni Vives, *SMART City Barcelona: The Catalan Quest to Improve Future Urban Living.*

GERNIKA
Genealogy of a Lie

XABIER A. IRUJO

Cañada Blanch Centre
for Contemporary
Spanish Studies

sussex
ACADEMIC
PRESS
Brighton • Chicago • Toronto

2 4 6 8 10 9 7 5 3 1

First published 2019 in Great Britain by
SUSSEX ACADEMIC PRESS
PO Box 139
Eastbourne BN24 9BP

Distributed in North America by
Independent Publishers Group
814 N. Franklin Street
Chicago, IL 60610

Published in collaboration with the Cañada Blanch Centre for Contemporary Spanish Studies, London School of Economics.

British Library Cataloguing in Publication Data
A CIP catalogue record for this book is available from the British Library.

Library of Congress Cataloging-in-Publication Data
Names: Irujo Ametzaga, Xabier, author.
Title: Gernika : genealogy of a lie / Xabier A. Irujo.
Description: Brighton ; Chicago : Sussex Academic Press, 2019. | Series:
   The Cañada Blanch/Sussex Academic studies on contemporary Spain |
Includes bibliographical references and index.
Identifiers: LCCN 2019008371 | ISBN 9781845199753 (pbk : alk. paper)
Subjects: LCSH: Guernica (Spain)—History—Bombardment, 1937—
   Historiography. | Truthfulness and falsehood—Political aspects—
   Spain—History—20th century. | Spain—History—Civil War, 1936–
   1939—Atrocities.
Classification: LCC DP269.27.G8 I785 2019 | DDC 946.081/48—dc23
LC record available at https://lccn.loc.gov/2019008371

Typeset & designed by Sussex Academic Press, Brighton & Eastbourne.
Printed by TJ International, Padstow, Cornwall.

Contents

The Cañada Blanch Centre for Contemporary Spanish Studies

In the 1960s, the most important initiative in the cultural and academic relations between Spain and the United Kingdom was launched by a Valencian fruit importer in London. The creation by Vicente Cañada Blanch of the Anglo-Spanish Cultural Foundation has subsequently benefited large numbers of Spanish and British scholars at various levels. Thanks to the generosity of Vicente Cañada Blanch, thousands of Spanish schoolchildren have been educated at the secondary school in West London that bears his name. At the same time, many British and Spanish university students have benefited from the exchange scholarships which fostered cultural and scientific exchanges between the two countries. Some of the most important historical, artistic and literary work on Spanish topics to be produced in Great Britain was initially made possible by Cañada Blanch scholarships.

Vicente Cañada Blanch was, by inclination, a conservative. When his Foundation was created, the Franco regime was still in the plenitude of its power. Nevertheless, the keynote of the Foundation's activities was always a complete open-mindedness on political issues. This was reflected in the diversity of research projects supported by the Foundation, many of which, in Francoist Spain, would have been regarded as subversive. When the Dictator died, Don Vicente was in his seventy-fifth year. In the two decades following the death of the Dictator, although apparently indestructible, Don Vicente was obliged to husband his energies. Increasingly, the work of the Foundation was carried forward by Miguel Dols whose tireless and imaginative work in London was matched in Spain by that of José María Coll Comín. They were united in the Foundation's spirit of open-minded commitment to fostering research of high quality in pursuit of better Anglo-Spanish cultural relations. Throughout the 1990s, thanks to them, the role of the Foundation grew considerably.

In 1994, in collaboration with the London School of Economics, the

Foundation established the Príncipe de Asturias Chair of Contemporary Spanish History and the Cañada Blanch Centre for Contemporary Spanish Studies. It is the particular task of the Cañada Blanch Centre for Contemporary Spanish Studies to promote the understanding of twentieth-century Spain through research and teaching of contemporary Spanish history, politics, economy, sociology and culture. The Centre possesses a valuable library and archival centre for specialists in contemporary Spain. This work is carried on through the publications of the doctoral and post-doctoral researchers at the Centre itself and through the many seminars and lectures held at the London School of Economics. While the seminars are the province of the researchers, the lecture cycles have been the forum in which Spanish politicians have been able to address audiences in the United Kingdom.

Since 1998, the Cañada Blanch Centre has published a substantial number of books in collaboration with several different publishers on the subject of contemporary Spanish history and politics. An extremely fruitful partnership with Sussex Academic Press began in 2004. Full details and descriptions of the published works can be found on the Press website.

One of the achievements of the series has been the publication of numerous works on the Spanish Civil War, ranging from biographies of both important and lesser-known protagonists of the war to major works on the medical services and on the repression carried out by the Francoist forces. The present volume by the distinguished Basque historian Xabier Irujo complements the remarkable work by Martin Minchom, *Spain's Martyred Cities: From the Battle of Madrid to Picasso's Guernica* (2015). It distils his path-breaking work on the bombing of Gernika and makes its historical truth available to a wider audience.

Series Editor's Preface by Paul Preston

Franco's war effort in northern Spain was headed by General Emilio Mola. The organiser of the military coup of July 1936, he had proclaimed the need to spread terror: "We have to create the impression of mastery, eliminating without scruples or hesitation all those who do not think as we do." When his troops occupied the capital of Guipúzcoa, San Sebastián, in September 1936, the number of executions carried out there would be the highest carried out by the rebels in any Basque city. Among those executed were thirteen Basque priests. Father Alberto Onaindia, whose brother was one of the victims, said prophetically: "If this was how the army behaved with the Basque clergy, what would it be like for civilians!"

As long as the siege of Madrid was Franco's main obsession, the Basque front remained static until late March 1937. However, the Republican victory at Guadalajara on 20 March 1937 finally under-mined Franco's belief that he could win the war at Madrid. Mola was ordered to gather nearly 40,000 troops for an assault on the Basque Country, and he opened his campaign at the end of the month with a widely publicised threat: "If submission is not immediate, I will raze all Vizcaya to the ground, beginning with the industries of war. I have the means to do so." However, despite Mola's evident desire for a quick victory, the campaign was slower than either the rebels or their German allies cared for. Stern Basque resistance, coupled with steep, wooded hills and poor roads, held up the advance.

Mola enjoyed the air support of the German Condor Legion, whose Chief of Staff was Lieutenant-Colonel Wolfram von Richthofen, cousin of the 'Red Baron'. Von Richthofen, who was later to mastermind the Nazi invasion of Poland, used the Condor Legion to practice the tech-niques of coordinated ground and air attacks, dive-bombing and saturation bombing, which were later to be incorporated into the Second World War Blitzkrieg. A cold-bloodedly professional commander, von

Richthofen was committed to the use of terror. He advised Mola that "nothing is unreasonable that can further destroy enemy morale and quickly". On the night of 25 April, Mola had the rebel radio at Salamanca broadcast the following warning to the Basque people: "Franco is about to deliver a mighty blow against which all resistance is useless. Basques! Surrender now and your lives will be spared."

On the following afternoon, 26 April, which was a Monday and market day in the small town of Gernika, the Condor Legion struck. Gernika, which was of deep symbolic importance to the Basque people, was destroyed by sustained bomb attacks from 4:20 p.m. to 7:40 p.m. The scale of the atrocity was compounded by the barrage of lies broadcast by the rebels and their allies to deny any responsibility. The Australian Noel Monks was one of the first correspondents to reach the town and he was immediately recruited by Basque relief workers to help collect charred bodies: "Some of the soldiers were sobbing like children. There were flames and smoke and grit, and the smell of burning human flesh was nauseating. Houses were collapsing into the inferno."

George Steer, correspondent of *The Times* and the Scotsman Christopher Holme, arrived with Monks. Steer's report was published on 28 April:

> "Gernika, the most ancient town of the Basques and the centre of their cultural tradition, was completely destroyed by insurgent air raiders. The bombardment of this open town far behind the lines occupied precisely three hours and a quarter, during which a powerful fleet of aeroplanes consisting of three German types, Junkers and Heinkel bombers and Heinkel fighters, did not cease unloading on the town bombs weighing from 1,000 lb downwards and, it is calculated, more than 3,000 two-pounder aluminium incendiary projectiles. The fighters, meanwhile, plunged low from above the centre of the town to machine-gun those of the civilian population who had taken refuge."

Steer was a first-class war correspondent and his report, appearing in *The Times*, had the most damaging impact on Franco's cause. The rebel foreign press service, under the direction of Luis Bolín, went to great lengths to denigrate Steer's personal and professional integrity.

Within twelve hours of the bombing, at 7.00 a.m. on 27 April, Franco, backed by the Third Reich, denied that the bombing had taken place on the spurious grounds that no planes had flown on 26 April because of fog. The three journalists secured the weather reports for the previous days and it was confirmed that there had been no fog for a week in the Basque Country. Franco was lying. However, as Monks wrote later, "Then came the last straw, for me." All three had gone back to Bilbao where they were "listening to General Queipo de Llano make one of his vile broadcasts to the women of Madrid, telling them, in detail, what to expect from the Moors. Suddenly he switched to Guernica. "'That Señor Monks', he croaked. 'Don't believe what he writes of Guernica. All the time he was with Franco's forces he was drunk.' Up to then, I'd been a teetotaler all my life!"

The initial rebel denials were amplified into the claim that Gernika had been dynamited by the Basques themselves in order to fabricate an atrocity for propaganda purposes. So-called experts were sent to Gernika weeks afterwards, when the smell of burnt human flesh had been replaced by petrol dumped here and there among the ruins by General Mola's men in order to sustain the lie that "Gernika was set on fire wilfully by the Reds". Franco's denial was reproduced by the controlled media of the regimes of Franco, Salazar, Hitler and Mussolini. It remained the official truth within Spain until Franco's death in 1975. It was thus one of the longest lasting official lies in Western European contemporary history.

The decision to bomb Gernika was reached by the mutual agreement of Mola's staff and the staff of the German Condor Legion. The ultimate responsibility lay with Franco who had given both a free hand. Some 24 German bombers and about 19 fighters and at least 13 Italian fighters took part in the operation. This constituted approximately 20 percent of the aircraft available to General Franco in April 1937 in the whole of the Iberian Peninsula. Between 31 and 41 tons of explosive and incendiary bombs were dropped from 800 meters on the city centre, destroying 85.22 percent of the town's buildings and partially damaging the rest. Professor Irujo's rigorous study methodically demolishes the thirty principal lies about the bombing which are still being propounded today. As he shows, unfortunately for Bolín, there were too many reliable witnesses, among them Father Onaindia who was in the town on the day of the German attack.

It was not difficult to find out what had happened. Virginia Cowles, an American reporter, travelled extensively through rebel Spain and visited the remains of Gernika in the company of one of Bolín's press officers, Ignacio Rosalles.

"We arrived in Gernika to find it a lonely chaos of timber and brick, like an ancient civilisation in process of being excavated. There were only three or four people in the streets. An old man was clearing away debris. Accompanied by Rosalles, my official escort, I went up to him and asked if he had been in the town during the destruction. He nodded his head and, when I asked what had happened, waved his arms in the air and declared that the sky had been black with planes – 'Aviones', he said, 'Italianos y alemanes.' Rosalles was astonished. 'Gernika was burned,' he contradicted heatedly. The old man, however, stuck to his point, insisting that after a four-hour bombardment there was little left to burn. Rosalles moved me away. 'He's a red', he explained indignantly. A couple of days later, we were talking to some staff officers. Rosalles described our drive along the coast and told them of the incident at Gernika. 'The town was full of reds', he said. 'They tried to tell us it was bombed, not burnt.' The tall staff officer replied: 'But of course it was bombed. We bombed it and bombed it and bombed it, and bueno, why not?' Rosalles looked astonished, and when we were back in the car again he said, 'I don't think I would write about that if I were you.' "

As Xabier Irujo demonstrates, the myth of the Basque dynamiters was counter-productive. Had the Nationalist authorities taken the same line as the nonchalant staff officer, then the bombing might have been dismissed as a regrettable consequence of war. As it was, the controversy made it a central symbol of the war, immortalised in the title of the painting by Pablo Picasso. As another Sussex volume, Martin Minchom's *Spain's Martyred Cities*, has demonstrated, the painting had its origins more in the bombing of Madrid and the occupation of Picasso's home town, Málaga, than with what happened at Gernika.

The Basque Government registered 1,654 deaths, although the Basque authorities reported that many more people lost their lives there whose bodies could not be rescued, identified, registered or properly buried. However, ignoring evidence compiled by Professor Irujo and others, more than eighty years after the attack, there are historians who claim that only between 100 to 250 people lost their lives in Gernika. The mayor of Gernika, José Labauria, said that, in the shelter of Andra Mari Street alone, 450 had died. The work of removing rubble from the city centre did not begin until February 1939 and it had not still not been cleared by the end of 1941. In the course of removing more than 180,000 tons of rubble, the Francoist authorities did not record the excavation of any body and registered no deaths.

That Gernika was destroyed by the German Condor Legion is no longer open to any doubt. Moreover, it is this fact which gives the event its military significance, for the town was the first in the world's history to have been entirely destroyed by aerial bombing. The only controversy which remains in relation to the atrocity is whether it was carried out at the behest of the Nationalist high command, or on the initiative of the Nazis. The late Dr Herbert Southworth, author of a path-breaking study of destruction of Gernika, reached the unequivocal conclusion that the town was destroyed by explosive and incendiary bombs dropped from aircraft of the Condor Legion piloted by Germans, a bombing undertaken at the request of the Nationalist high command in order to destroy Basque morale and undermine the defence of Bilbao.

That the entire operation was an experiment in terror designed to cause the greatest possible number of civilian victims could be deduced from the choice of projectiles – a combination of explosive bombs and light incendiaries. Professor Irujo has now confirmed beyond all doubt the murderous intent of the attackers. He has demonstrated that the first targets were the municipal water tanks and the fire-station precisely in order to prevent the fires being put out. Moreover, as he shows, terrified civilians who fled to the surrounding fields were herded back into the town by the machine-gun strafing of Heinkel He 51 fighters that circled the town in what Richthofen called 'the ring of fire' (*Feuerring*). Von Richthofen, an austerely efficient man, had access to the Henschel Hs 123 dive bomber, by far the most suitable aircraft in existence on the Basque front. Yet he chose not to use it. Even so, eye-witnesses have testified to the fact that the conventional bombers which he did use flew low enough to have been able to drop bombs with some accuracy. However, they flew too wide apart for them to have been concentrating on a specific target. Moreover, the weight of bombs dropped on Guernica was the equivalent of half of the tonnage dropped by the entire Condor Legion on the crucial opening day of the campaign when it was necessary to make an early break-through. In fact, it seems that under the Renteria bridge was by far the safest place to be in Guernica during the bombing.

This book distils Professor Irujo's substantial work in elucidating further the truth of what happened in Gernika on April 26, 1937. His research builds on a long tradition of uncovering the truth that was started by Noel Monks, George Steer and Christopher Holme on the day

Gernika was bombed. That tradition was consolidated by Herbert Southworth and Ángel Viñas, and advanced considerably by Irujo's now classic 2012 book *El Gernika de Richthofen*. The present volume concentrates on exposing the lies and myths that have stood in the way of a truthful examination of the motivation, the implementation and the consequences of the tragedy. In that sense, his work has an ethical dimension that casts its light beyond the tragic story of the bombing of Gernika and the death of civilians during the war in the Basque Country. It has implications for all those who are working to recover the historical memory of the victims of atrocities in all parts of the world.

Author's Preface

On April 26, 1937, a weekly market day, a minimum of 27 bombers and 32 fighters departed from the aerodromes of Burgos, Soria, Gasteiz, and possibly also Lasarte, attacked Gernika between 4:20 p.m. and 7:40 p.m. They dropped between 31 and 46 tons of explosive and incendiary bombs on the city center. The desolation was absolute: 85.22 percent of the buildings in the town were totally destroyed, and 99 percent were damaged. There were more than 2,000 deaths among a population of the approximately 10,000 to 12,000 civilians who were in the urban area, an area of less than one square kilometer.[1]

One of the pilots who participated in the attack was Hans J. Wadel, a 23-year-old architect born in Silesia. As an amateur aviator, his whole life was going to take a dramatic turn in just one month. In April 1937 he volunteered at one of the 2,800 offices of the Detlev-Rohwedder-Haus on Wilhelmstrasse street in Berlin. In 1936, after two years of construction the headquarters of the Luftwaffe, designed by Air Minister Hermann Göring, became the largest office building in the world. In a matter of minutes Wandel was hired, with a salary of 600 pesetas a month (about $600) plus all expenses and a bonus when he returned to Germany. On April 22 he took off on a commercial flight from the Tempelhof airport in Berlin and arrived in Seville via Rome a day later.

Two days later he was assigned a Heinkel He 51 ground-attack aircraft. Nicknamed the Gnome, Wandel was ordered to practice machine-gun fire against real targets at 900, 600, and 500 meters of altitude for three days.[2] After this short training, on April 25 he was transferred to Gasteiz, where he joined the two fighter squadrons led by Harro Harder and Douglas Pitcairn.[3] And four days after his arrival to the war, he participated in the machine-gunning of civilians in Gernika, putting into practice what he had learned.

On May 13, when he was recording the results of the bombing and strafing, a Basque soldier (*gudari*) shot him down. Wandel parachuted out of his damaged plane and as he descended he could see a group of soldiers approaching. He wisely decided to surrender without a fight and released his pistol from the air. When he was captured the *gudari* that seized him examined his wallet where he kept his identity documents. Among them he had a postcard addressed to his girlfriend Else, which read: "Spain is a magnificent country. We can destroy it in a few weeks. Yesterday we buried a village [Gernika]."[4]

At his trial, Wandel admitted that he had escorted the German bombers in their raid against "Basque pine forests with incendiary bombs."[5] But he did not want to admit that he had participated in the bombing of Gernika. One of the Basque soldiers who was guarding him saw how he altered his flight logbook and took it from him. He was trying to erase the word "Gernika" from it. Wandel explained to the court that he had underlined the word so that everyone who read his log would know that he had participated in the bombing. Obviously, he was lying. He finally confessed his participation in the crime and was sentenced to death by the Basque court of justice.[6]

Lies are inherent to crime. This crime generated a cascade of lies beginning on the morning of April 27 when Franco ordered the bombing be denied and the "Reds" be accused of having burned the city. Just hours after the denial order was issued, the bombing of Gernika became one of the most prominent and long-lasting official lies of the 20th century in Europe. The news of the bombing and the subsequent denial of the facts by the three dictatorships involved in the atrocity saturated the front pages of the European and American press. Today the bombing is considered an icon of terror bombing and denial. The outline below presents, schematically, the genealogy of the lie about the bombing of Gernika:

1. Franco ordered a double lie: Denial of the bombing and accusing the "Reds" of having set Gernika afire.
2. This version was reproduced in the media of the regimes involved in the events – Franco's Spain, Nazi Germany, and Fascist Italy.
3. Franco ordered that two official narratives be written (the Machimbarrena and Herrán Reports) in an attempt to provide fake documentation and give a scientific character to the official version.
4. The spreading of the news about the fire generated new versions of the facts, often incompatible and inconsistent.
5. The dictatorship censored the access to the truth for forty years

and imposed its official and alternative truth, calling it "the only truth."

6. By virtue of the enduring repression by the Franco regime, the official lie crystallized and generated an active reductionist/revisionist stream of thought that tends to repeat or reenact the topics generated during the four decades of dictatorship.

The first lie was an order. And during forty years of dictatorship, even after the end of World War II and the Nuremberg trials, the official truth of the regime was that the Basques had burnt down Gernika with gasoline. This original version enabled the blatant denial that Gernika had ever been bombed, and this original negationism, protected by the regime's propaganda machine, has given rise to reductionism or the attempt to minimize each and every one of the aspects of the bombing (the nature of the attack, the number of aircraft that participated, the tonnage of bombs dropped, the time of flight over Gernika, the flight height, and many other minor details). And this reductionism or revisionism is alive and well today.

Wandel lied to save his life before the judge who sentenced him to death; Franco lied to protect the interests of the coup that instigated the war, before an international audience, as "a Crusade of true Spain against the Godless."[7] Lies differ according to their origins, and there are many ways to denaturalize the truth, many reasons to cheat, and various strategies to do so. Generically speaking, lies are polyhedral.

The subject of this book is "the official lie" (political or diplomatic) and the "historiographical lie" (historical fraud). In 1977 Herbert Southworth published *Guernica! Guernica! A Study of Journalism, Diplomacy, Propaganda, and History*, a key piece elucidating the origin of denialism and reductionism concerning the bombing of Gernika. In 2013 the Comares publishing house issued a second edition in Spanish with an epilogue by Ángel Viñas. More than forty years after this classic on the history of the bombing saw light, *Gernika: Genealogy of a Lie* follows the same line, trying to unravel the dense network of falsehoods around the bombing and the logic that transcends it. It is not an analysis and description of the bombing but of its denial. A lie does not exist by itself but rather through deformation of the truth and, therefore, if there were something that we refer to as "true and verifiable facts," there would be neither fraud nor fiction. From this perspective, lies are only a mirror of truth, but an aberrant mirror.

Some philosophers have gone further, stating that it is impossible for us to know the truth, so that everything is an illusion. Napoleon Bonaparte applied this skeptical view to the realm of humanities and social sciences by stating that historical narrative is a set of agreed-upon lies. Perhaps, but the truth or the historiographic lie is subject to the deontology of this scientific discipline, and the application of these methodological principles is what distinguishes an unfounded and unscientific opinion from the historical criterion based on documents and judgment.

Contrary to appearances, the strategies and the logic on which the historical lie is based are not very versatile. As Adam Jones expressed in 2011, most of the falsehoods about a historical event can be classified into eight groups, eight type ideas or syllogisms that are repeated whenever an atrocity has become a historiographical battlefield. And all of them are present in the reductionist literature around the bombing of Gernika:[8]

1. "Nobody gave the order, there was no central command."
2. "It was not an atrocity."
3. "It was not intended to do that: it was an accident."
4. "It is war; these things happen, and worse things have happened."
5. "There were not so many people at that particular time and place."
6. "No one died."
7. We are not monsters: we would not be able to do something like that.
8. "Being innocent, we have been blamed for everything."

In addition to these background syllogisms, filtered among the more than thirty lies demonstrated in this book, reductionism is methodologically deficient. Reductionist or revisionist literature bases its versions of the truth on documents that lack credibility, in this case the reports written by the totalitarian regimes involved in the event, such as the information of the Scientific Section of the Luftwaffe or the Machimbarrena and Herrán Reports written by order of the Franco regime. At the same time, revisionist literature systematically omits or discredits oral testimonies and documents produced by international reporters and observers, without the slightest documentary support or scientific criterion. Methodologically and ethically, this is totally inappropriate.

Some of the most outstanding features of the historiographic lie that I try to unveil are the following:

1. Lies arise from a real and concrete fact, as an explanation of the truth.
2. Lies are part of a genealogical chain of falsehoods.
3. Lies reproduce, grow, and mutate.
4. Lies are transmitted, spread, and multiplied easily.
5. Unlike the truth, lies take on various forms depending on the light provided by the material evidence.
6. Lying is capricious.
7. Lying may easily lead to another lie, and this later lie to the subsequent truth.
8. Lies are overbearing and petulant.
9. Lies are often accompanied by insults.

Like matter dissolved in a liquid, lies hold the magnitude of density. It is extraordinary to observe the capacity for dissolution of some historical texts. For example, the letter that Colonel Wolfram von Richthofen wrote to General Alfredo Kindelán in May 1937 contains no less than 14 falsehoods diluted in 300 words (21.42 words per falsehood). The report of the Scientific Section of the Luftwaffe contains 18 falsehoods (in italics) in a text of 184 words (10.22 w/f):

> On April 26 an aviation attack was ordered *against the bridge and the road junction to the east of Guernica,* which had to be difficult *and was carried out by nine planes* from *2,300 m altitude, in a single flight. Nine bombs of 250 kilos* and *114 of 50 kilos,* altogether *7,950 kilos* were thrown. The inspection revealed that the bridge had not received any impact. *Vision was totally insufficient,* because the city was engulfed in flames and smoke. *This bombing was used by the entire hostile world press as a pretext to blame especially German units for the destruction of the city. The issue was exploited in order to produce the most violent state of mind.* All the aviators, *following orders,* had nevertheless *respected the place.* Instead, *the Reds turned it into a pile of ruins, according to a plan of fires and blowing.* This is also clear from the fact that the attacking units *faced great obstacles in their vision,* due to the thick smoke produced by *the already burned* city.[9]

The order to lie issued by Franco on April 27, 1937, at dawn, which is the source of all the falsehoods that this book deals with, contains a density of falsehoods that is difficult to reach: Eleven lies in 50 words (4.54 w/f).

Lies are born, develop, and die, and so does truth. And sometimes lies crystallize, surviving truth as fossils. Reviewing historical facts with objectivity and transmitting the memory of the most tragic events in human history is one of our responsibilities as historians, but also as members of the human family, because no matter how painful the truth may be, it will always be less than the grief that lies and deceit impose on the victims.

People who died in the bombing lost their lives, but their memory must be rescued and honored. That is truth for all victims in all human conflicts.

The Illustrations

All illustrations are courtesy of the Documentation Center of the Bombing of Gernika, Foru Plaza 1, 48300 Gernika-Lumo (Bizkaia).

The cover illustrations: Following General Franco's orders to deny that the Rebel aviation had bombed Gernika, General Gonzalo Queipo de Llano, broadcasting from from Radio Sevilla, was one of the first persons to deny that Gernika had been bombed. He is the image of the lie.

The 23 photographs, which are place after page 60, are contextual to the chapters as detailed below

The Gernika Prize
for Peace and Reconciliation

The city council of Gernika has awarded the 2019 Gernika Prize for Peace and Reconciliation to historians Xabier Irujo, Paul Preston, and Angel Viñas.

These awards are granted every April 26 by the City Council of Gernika to commemorate events of the bombing that in 1937 ravaged the city. Previous awardees of this prize were Nobel Peace Prize recipient Adolfo Pérez Esquivel (2007), the former president of Germany, Roman Herzog (2012), the former president of Uruguay, José Mujica (2016), and the former president of Colombia, Juan M. Santos Calderon (2017).

The 2019 awards to the named historians relate to their work and publications that bring to light the truth of the bombing of Gernika through scientific historiographic criteria and method. Their work promotes "ethics and responsibility" in the recovery of historical memory.

GERNIKA

Genealogy of a Lie

Chapter 1

Italy and Germany did not intervene

Few people wanted war in Europe in the summer of 1936. The coalition of the French Front Populaire, led by the president of the council of ministers, Léon Blum, had strong political links with Manuel Azaña's Popular Front of in Spain, but after the coup d'état of July 1936 and the eruption of war, this alliance challenged peace in the French Republic. At the beginning of August, the German ambassador in Paris, Johannes Welczeck, recalled that in 1871 an internal Spanish political conflict had already ended in a war between Germany and France.[1] Blum was alarmed at the risk of triggering a conflict at a European or even global level and, despite political ties and ideological sympathies, decided to isolate his government. In early August Blum proposed to the British government to create a system of non-intervention that prohibited the export and transit of arms and ammunition to either of the two sides in the Iberian Peninsula.

On August 4, the French prime minister received British approval. The plan was simple: both countries would declare themselves "neutral" in relation to "the Spanish conflict" and would invite Germany, Italy, and the Soviet Union to join the system of non-intervention regarding the Spanish "internal" conflict. Both the British and the French administrations were aware that Hitler and Mussolini had already sent war material in aid of Franco but, in line with the policy of appeasement, understood that they could control and even limit German and Italian military aid and, fundamentally, avoid the outbreak of a new world war or at least delay its beginning. The price of this strategy was that the Spanish Republic, without the ability to access the international weapons market, would collapse before the coup; the rebels, of course, could receive not only weapons and logistical support, but also troops from Germany and Italy.

In fact, the Non-intervention Pact convinced Mussolini, and later Hitler, to openly intervene in the war in favor of Franco. When on July 30, 1936, the Italian intelligence service leaked news that the French, British, and Soviet governments had decided to remain neutral in the conflict, Mussolini decided to intervene massively, since the intervention of the enemies of the Republic assured victory for the plotters who would enjoy the full assistance of the future Axis powers, in flagrant violation of the said pact.[2] As U.S. Ambassador to the Spanish Republic Claude G. Bowers indicated, "The Non-intervention Pact was proving itself a dishonest farce. The Fascist powers fought just openly, defiantly, with arms; most of the democracies fought just as effectively, if unconsciously, as collaborationists of the Fascist under the mocking cloak of 'non-intervention.'"[3]

At the beginning of September 1936, twenty-seven European governments had agreed to prohibit in their respective countries sending war material to either side and to inform each other of the measures taken to stop the arms trade with the two aforementioned parties. But everything was a deception. In fact, on August 17, twenty-two days before joining the non-intervention system, Germany had already sent war material and troops to Franco and, starting in November would significantly increase the presence of troops through the creation of the Condor Legion, a special unit of the Luftwaffe that was constantly maintained between the end of 1936 and the beginning of 1939 with a total of 5,000 soldiers equipped and on the warpath. As noted by British reporter George L. Steer, when the German aviator Karl G. Schmidt was captured on January 4, 1937, after his Junkers Ju 52 was shot down while bombing Bilbao, the *gudaris* who apprehended him found that his silk parachute had been manufactured in Germany at an interesting date: twenty-four hours before Hitler's adoption of the non-intervention agreement.

In an exercise of political cynicism, the Italian government even approved royal decree law no. 562 of April 10, 1937, which comprised seventeen dense articles on the prohibition of transporting troops or ammunition on Italian ships to the Iberian Peninsula and on the control schemes to which the said vessels would be committed.[4] By then Italy had a minimum of 50,000 men in the theater of operations, equipped with bombers, fighters, warships, submarines, tanks, and all kinds of heavy weapons.

As Bowers pointed out, the Non-intervention Pact was not a pact but rather a commitment, since there was never a written or official copy of it and it was never signed; its purpose was not non-intervention but rather to manage and control the German and Italian intervention in order to avoid a world war. All administrations were aware that Germany and Italy were sending troops and war material to the theater of operations. In fact, the British government had intercepted all internal communications of the Italian administration so that it had specific, detailed, and exhaustive information about each and every one of the shipments of troops and war material assigned to the war. Day by day and transport to transport, the British government had accurate information as to the exact number of men, rifles, and even of cartridges that were sent in each one of the merchant ships that were chartered between August of 1936 and the end of the war in the spring of 1939.

But the countries involved decided to lie.

The Non-intervention Committee tacitly chose not to establish a system of sanctions for those governments that violated the agreement, nor even to mention the possibility of taking cases of transgression of the agreement to the League of Nations for arbitration. In fact, protests or accusations of transgression were reduced to the crossing of private notes from the British embassies in Rome or Berlin to the Italian or German administrations on the continual transfer of troops to the war, or to private discussions within the committee between the Secretary of the Foreign Office Anthony Eden and the German ambassador in London, Joachim von Ribbentrop, or the Italian delegate Dino Grandi.[5] The government of the Spanish Republic repeatedly raised breach of the Non-intervention Pact before the League of Nations, but these claims were dismissed on the grounds that they were not properly "verified." Thus, for example, Minister of State Julio Álvarez del Vayo brought before the League of Nations on September 27 and November 27, 1936, and again on March 13, 1937, two reports with photographs and documentary evidence of the presence of German and Italian troops in the war, among them the 46-page pamphlet entitled *Italian Aggression: Documents Taken to the Italian Units in the Action of Guadalajara.*[6] Moreover, after the disaster of the battle of Guadalajara in March 1937, the Spanish Foreign Ministry distributed hundreds of photographs of Italian troops in Republican prisons, armaments and , ammunition, and other incontestable pieces of evidence. In fact, from the beginning of the war in July 1936 to May 1938, a total of 144 German and Italian pilots were captured, but the League of Nations avoided any resolution with respect to the evidences presented.

Franco lied, as did Generals Emilio Mola and Gonzalo Queipo de Llano and many other military leaders, diplomats, and politicians involved in sending troops and war material to the coup participants, but the political leaders of the Western democracies that were part of the non-intervention system were also forced to lie to their own parliaments and their own people for three years. When, after the bombing of Gernika, Ribbentrop expressed to Eden that the British press had made "incorrect and tendentious accusations" about the participation of German planes in the event, Eden replied that the government lacked accurate information about what had taken place in Gernika because the Foreign Office reports were inconsistent and based on British media articles.[7] But the truth is that Eden and Sir Henry G. Chilton, British ambassador to the Spanish Republic, had in their hands a conclusive report by Ralph C. Stevenson, British Consul in Bilbao, written on May 4.[8] Stevenson went personally to Gernika in the early hours of April 27 when the city was still burning and reported that it had been destroyed by some fifty planes launching explosive and incendiary bombs for three and a half hours and that civilians had been ruthlessly machine-gunned by combat aircraft. Eden intentionally lied to Ribbentrop, but also to the House of Commons, in stating that he had no conclusive data, even though an unexploded incendiary bomb that had been sent from Gernika was in the hands of the British authorities. And, above all, he exhorted Ribbentrop to make an "adequate" statement denying German participation in the bombing to the British press.[9]

Émile Vandervelde, Minister of Health of the Belgian government, said that "the Non-intervention committee has eyes to play blind and ears to play deaf."[10] It is interesting to read the Non-intervention Committee minutes and to realize that it is possible to discuss and write dozens of volumes of records for three years without saying anything.[11] Everyone played that macabre game. General Emilio Mola, head of the Army of the North, swore on his honor in January 1937 that there were no German volunteers in the war because "such is the spirit of national Spain and the bravery of its soldiers, that we have defeated our adversaries and we continue to overcome them, and we will impose peace on them. And we will impose it without German volunteers because we do not have them or need them. If the Red Command or any other country that wishes it points to a single German infantry company in the national Army, I swear on my honor that I will surrender without conditions to my former captain and expert electric power poacher, the red comrade Miaja . . . "[12] Richthofen, chief of staff of the Condor Legion, wrote ironically that "the irritation provoked by the German bombings is, of course, completely unjustified, in that here there are exclusively Spanish troops!"[13] The press controlled by the rebel government also stressed the idea that "there is no German or foreign aviation in National Spain. There is Spanish aviation, noble and heroic Spanish aviation, which has to fight continuously against red aircraft, which are Russian and French navigated by foreign aviators."[14]

For three long years, all the European administrations referred to the pilots of the Condor Legion and the Italian troops as "volunteers," with the world press maintaining the fiction that neither Italy nor Germany were at war with the Spanish Republic. Joachim von Ribbentrop himself, one of the main architects of the non-intervention system, wrote in his memoirs that "a better name for the committee would have been Intervention committee," since its members focused their efforts on defending or silencing news about the international participation in the war and favoring and facilitating Italian and German participation.[15] In short, as Charles Maurice de Talleyrand pointed out more than a century earlier, non-intervention is a political and metaphysical formula that involves almost exactly the same thing as intervention. Faced with this tragic comedy and the plethora of lies in the international press, the British journalist Claud Cockburn recommended his readers not believe anything "until it was officially denied."

Chapter 2

It was a civil and Spanish war

The immediate consequence of accepting the non-intervention farce was that neither Italy nor Germany nor Portugal nor the kingdom of Morocco was intervening or militarily assisting the rebels in the context of a war that the Non-intervention Committee emphatically referred to as "civil and Spanish." However, although at the beginning the conflict began as a confrontation between two Spanish political blocs, it was much more than a war. It became a campaign of genocide and very soon transcended that of a civil and Spanish conflagration.

The Republican administration repeatedly declared through its official representatives before the Assembly of the League of Nations that the military participation of outside forces made it into an international war. The Minister of State, Julio Álvarez del Vayo, repeatedly condemned the active participation of Germany and Italy, and on September 27, 1936 forwarded to the General Secretariat of the League of Nations a series of documents with graphic and detailed information about the repeated violations of the Non-intervention Pact among the Italian, German, and Portuguese regimes.[1]

Neither Hitler nor Mussolini ever believed that it was a civil conflict. Indeed, from the moment they determined that their participation should be massive and decisive, both leaders understood that this war was an international conflagration to save Europe from the Bolshevik threat and from British hegemony. Despite the fact that Italy did not participate officially, the Italian press emphatically and without concealment emphasized the actions of the Fascist troops, often providing commentary and photographic evidence. In the summer of 1937, when the spring campaign ended in the Basque Country, the Italian government announced that 325 Italian soldiers had lost their lives and 1,676 had been injured.[2] The government also published the list of ten Italian generals in command of the troops that had occupied Santander.

Cardinal Gomá, "the highest representative of the Spanish ecclesiastical hierarchy"[3] and one of the main leaders of the uprising, said bluntly that it was not a civil war but a struggle for "the salvation of Europe." According to the Cardinal, the conflict appeared as a purely civil war only because it was fought on Spanish soil and by the Spaniards themselves but he recognized in it the spirit of a true crusade for Catholicism."[4] And he concluded unambiguously: "Is the Spanish war a civil war? It is not; it is a struggle of the godless [. . .] against the true Spain, against the Catholic religion."[5] The point he is making is that the military personnel who orchestrated the coup d'état understood from the outset that the participation of the totalitarian powers in the conflict would benefit them, so they requested international participation in the conflict.

At the League of Nations, very few members doubted the international character of the conflict. Isidro Fabela, delegate from Mexico, stressed that it was not a civil and Spanish conflict, but a military rebellion against a legitimately constituted government, representative of the popular will, and supported by foreign powers. Fabela added that the non-intervention system only prolonged a conflict that could lead, as it did in 1939, to the Second World War.[6]

Few people in the British administration believed it was a civil and Spanish war, and that understanding was precisely what motivated the creation of the Non-intervention Committee. A year after the bombing of Gernika, the British and Italian governments, both committee members, signed the so-called Easter Accords on April 16, 1938, through which the British government demanded withdrawal of troops from the Iberian Peninsula at the end of the war in exchange for British recognition of Italian sovereignty over Abyssinia.[7] After lying to the press, to his parliament, and his people for more than two years, Eden felt embarrassed and resigned, although he was quickly replaced by Lord Halifax, who later signed the Treaty of Munich with Germany on September 29, 1938.

In the United States, officials also dismissed the Non-intervention Committee's claim that the conflict was purely civil and Spanish. As noted in a report by the U.S. military intelligence division of December 1937, General Franco's insurrection soon acquired the dimensions and nature of a miniature world war.[8] After the bombing of Gernika, Congressman Jerry J. O'Connell called the attention of Secretary of State Cordel Hull to the Gernika massacre, which was, according to his statement, reported by all foreign correspondents of accredited newspapers as the work of German aircraft, bombs, and pilots. O'Connell requested the State Department to officially acknowledge what in his view was public and notorious, that is, "that Germany and Italy are in fact belligerents in the war of invasion now going on in Spain."[9] Hull agreed with Nevada Senator Key Pittman, chairman of the Senate Foreign Relations Committee since 1933, who had argued that there was no evidence that Germany or Italy were participating in the war.

But the fact is that Hull was well informed from the letters, notes, telegrams, and general documentation that Bowers sent him from the U.S. embassy in Hendaia. Bowers sent at least forty documents on the participation of German and Italian troops in the war from January 1937 to May 19, some of them written by Bowers himself and others by William C. Bullitt, U.S. ambassador to the French Republic. Many of them expressed unequivocally terms that "the French government has positive information that Italians now have 50,000 soldiers in Spain" and that "two days ago six ships left Naples and Gaeta carrying more troops and ammunition and that at the end of this week there would be more than 60,000 Italian troops in Spain."[10] There was also information available on the disembarkation of no fewer than 3,000 German troops from Bavaria on Spanish territory on January 10, 1937. Bowers had written to Hull in these terms: "Now with a full knowledge that as many as 17,000 German and Italian soldiers landed at Cadiz within two weeks, beginning Christmas week, the British policy is to shut off 'volunteers' [. . .] and I shall be much astonished if anything is done that will stop Germany and Italy from continuing to send in soldiers."[11]

Claude Bowers repeatedly expressed his conviction that the war was not a civil conflict, and in his memoirs he stated categorically that he viewed the Spanish conflict a prologue to the Second World War: "It was just clear that it was not a 'civil war' in the usual meaning of the term, but a war of aggression openly waged by Hitler and Mussolini."[12] Bowers added, in a section entitled "A War of Foreigners," that the weight of the campaign was falling on foreign soldiers, including Moroccan, German, and Italian troops. In reference to the air force, he also declared that the Germans, due to advantages in arms, training, and ammunition, had assumed leadership over many aspects of the air war. The U.S. ambassador to Rome, William Phillips, also informed Hull repeatedly about Mussolini's substantial aid to the rebels, both in terms of supplies and manpower.[13] On May 29, the State Department received a detailed report from Phillips about the bombing of Gernika, stating that the German Luftwaffe was primarily responsible for the massacre. The Spanish Republican embassy sent a second report to Washington on June 12.[14]

In response to Hull's position, Senator O'Connell responded: "No evidence! Mr. Speaker, I ask you, what is the meaning of 'evidence' in the vocabulary of the State Department? The correspondents of many newspapers both for this country and for England signed their names to stories which recited in detail the 'evidence' the State Department chooses to ignore. One of those correspondents, G. L. Steer, cabled to the *New York Times* from Bilbao on April 28. I have seen and measured the enormous bomb holes at Guernica, which, since I passed through the towns the day before, I can testify were not there then. Unexploded German aluminum incendiary bombs found in Guernica were marked 'Rheindorf Factory, 1936'. The types of German airplanes employed were the Junkers Ju 52/3M heavy bombers, Heinkel He 111 medium-fast bombers, and Heinkel He 51 pursuit planes. Steer went on to quote statements of German pilots who, when captured early in April, admitted that the insurgent airplanes are "manned entirely by German pilots, while nearly all the crews are German. It seems that the State Department does not regard reports by responsible eyewitnesses as 'evidence'. But to the man on the street evidence that Germany and Italy are engaged in the most brutal slaughter of all history appears incontrovertible."[15]

However, Hull and Pittman continued to lie. Hull was awarded the Nobel Peace Prize in 1945.

In response to the bombing of Gernika, on June 2, 1937, a group of seven congressmen, led by Jerry O'Connell and John T. Bernard, sent a letter to Secretary of State Hull asking to enforce the resolution[16] approved by Congress, by virtue of which the president should proclaim Italy and Germany belligerent states at war with the Spanish Republic, as described in the Neutrality Act of 1937, and that, consequently, this law should apply to these countries.[17] The British embassy in Washington pressed the Roosevelt administration not to do so. Roosevelt reluctantly accepted the British demand but, in the course of his famous speech of October 5, 1937, in Chicago, he proposed establishing "a quarantine of aggressor nations" as an alternative to neutrality and the system of non-intervention, a request welcomed by the Spanish Prime Minister Juan Negrín.[18] The president's speech did not convince the isolationist majority in Congress, who understood that this was a problem generated in Europe among Europeans, but the German ambassador in Washington telegraphed Berlin stating that it was imprudent to count on American isolationism for long.[19] He was right. As Bowers predicted, four years later the United States was at war with Italy and Germany.

German and Italian intervention was not only fundamental, but decisive. Eighty-nine percent of Franco's air force in April 1937 was of German and Italian origin. On August 27, after the capture of Santander, the *Giornale d'Italia* published on its front page that "General Franco has declared to the world that today's victory is largely an Italian victory; a victory of the legionaries and their fascist leaders."[20] Lieutenant-Colonel Bruno Montanari concluded that without the participation of the Italian and German air units Franco would not have won the war;[21] indeed, both General Blomberg and Mussolini had no choice but to admit in June 1937 that the fall of Bilbao was due mainly to the actions of the German bombers.[22] Hitler himself reminded Franco that he should erect a monument to the Junkers Ju 52, to whom he owed victory, and declared[23] that "one thing is quite certain. People speak of an intervention from Heaven which decided the civil war in favor of Franco; perhaps so – but it was not an intervention on the part of the madam styled the Mother of God, who has recently been honored with a Field Marshal's baton, but the intervention of the German General von Richthofen and the bombs of his squadrons rained from the heavens that decided the issue."[24]

But despite all the above explanations, the term "Spanish Civil War" coined at the Non-intervention Committee is used by most authors and has been incorporated into the textbooks in more than twenty languages.

Chapter 3

No market was held in Gernika

Revisionist literature commonly minimizes the number of potential victims. In the case of the bombing of Gernika, it has been alleged that on Monday, April 26, the weekly market was not held and that, therefore, there was practically no one in the town and consequently the number of victims would have been small.

This issue was raised early; specifically, this is the twelfth conclusion of the Herrán Report, dated in Burgos, September 1937. The report was requested by the Duke of Alba, Franco's official representative in London, to demonstrate "scientifically" that Gernika had been set on fire: "The Basque Government had decreed the evacuation of Guernica for Monday the 26th. This is testified by Don Alberto Onaindia, Canon of the Cathedral of Valladolid, a native of Biscay, in some declarations which were published on page 3 of the pamphlet, Guernica, issued by the Basque Government [. . .]. There is no doubt that the secret order for the evacuation, given by the Basque Government, had been broadcast abroad and that those who knew of it attempted to fly to safety."[1]

There is no documentary evidence of any of these claims. A brochure entitled *Guernica* includes the testimony of Canon Onaindia, who says "that he had heard that the Basque Government had decided to evacuate Gernika."[2] It does not say at any time that an order for evacuation had been issued nor does it say that the evacuation was to take place on April 26. The evacuation referred to by Onaindia had been underway since the beginning of the war, town after town, village after village, before the entrance of the rebel troops in occupied places. The population fled for fear of reprisals. Moreover, later Onaindia stated that "since it was a market day, there were many neighbors from the surrounding towns in Gernika."[3] After the bombing, Onaindia testified repeatedly that the weekly market was held and that there were many people in the town. More specifically, he estimated that some 12,000 people gathered in Gernika that afternoon.[4]

Even though the alleged order of evacuation was secret, the authors of the Herrán Report stated that the news leaked and was known by all the "red separatists." No documentary evidence supports the claim that "the destruction of Guernica was the climax of the evacuation order issued by the Basque Government for the 26th of April,"[5] and, logically, there is no record to date of any order to evacuate the town. Lacking documentation to support their hypothesis, the authors of the report reproduced the testimonies of a series of witnesses whose allegations should not be taken as historical sources, since the report was drafted by the Francoist authorities and therefore lacks credibility. Jesús Obieta, a thirty-year-old resident of Gernika, said that "certain families of Red Separationists left Guernica on the morning of the 26th, taking with them their household goods and valuables."[6] Pedro A. García Sarabia appeared in Bilbao on July 30, 1937, before the members of the Herrán Commission: "On being asked if he had any information as to whether the aeroplanes had scattered hand-bills or announcements of the bombing, the witness stated that after his return to Guernica, between the 10th and 19th May, he heard a rumour that handbills had been scattered on the morning of the 26th April, and that the families of active Red Separationists left the town."[7] Secundino Blasco, interrogated by the members of the Herrán Commission, also made reference to this "rumor."

In another passage contradicting the previous statements, Salustiano Olazabal said that everyone left Gernika and that therefore there was almost no one in the town by the afternoon: "Many others, like the industrial engineer Don Salustiano Olazabal Menarguez, on leaving their houses in the afternoon, noticed with astonishment that Guernica was almost empty. From time immemorial a very busy cattle fair was held every Monday at Guernica, but on that Monday neither the cattle nor the attendants at the fair were anywhere to be seen. Senor Menarguez visited the place where he generally met his friends every day and found that nearly all had disappeared. It is evident that the order for the evacuation of Guernica was an open secret, and that those who from previous experience knew of the consequences likely to ensue were most anxious to escape them."[8]

Thus, the Herrán Report disseminated the idea that the Basque government circulated the evacuation order among its supporters so they could save their lives and most their precious belongings and escape from the city before the Reds set it afire that afternoon. In fact, the authors of the Herrán Report concluded that the rebel aviators executed a light bombing of the village and that the Basque authorities took advantage of it, setting Gernika afire and blaming the rebels. The report does not explain, however, how the authorities of the Basque government knew that the coup leaders were going to bomb Gernika on the afternoon of April 26.

But, despite the inconsistencies of this viewpoint, Vicente Talón took it up again in 1978, under the title of "A fundamental witness." This missive stated that Francisco Lazkano was named by the Lehendakari (president) Jose A. Agirre "delegate of the Government in the market of Gernika" to organize the evacuation. According to the author, the revelation about Lazkano was sensational because "he suspended the market celebrated every Monday in Gernika, to which numerous farmers from the surroundings villages used to go to sell their products."[9] According to Talón, "the order was fulfilled by pickets of *gudaris* strategically placed on the roads to Bilbao, Bermeo, Lekeitio and Errigoiti and, as a result, many fair-goers were forced to return to their places of origin. Other visitors to the fair used secondary access roads to reach Gernika. Agirre also banned the Basque ball game scheduled for that afternoon and arranged, within the framework of these security measures, that all vehicles that did not have something specific to do with regard to the market leave the urban area and take shelter under the protective umbrella of the trees of the Paseo de los Tilos."[10]

Testimonies contradict this version of the facts presented above. Specifically and without being exhaustive, there are more than thirty-six direct testimonies from people who were in the market selling or buying products, which demonstrate beyond any reasonable doubt that in fact the market was held and very well attended.[11] To these thirty-six testimonies it is necessary to add those collected in 1996 by María J. Cava, María Silvestre, and Javier Arranz, who concluded that "it seems more than evident that, unquestionably, that Monday of 1937 the market was held as always."[12] Moreover, as many of these witnesses affirm, the Basque government arranged several trains to enable people in Bilbao to buy food at the market, given the critical shortage of food in the Basque capital.

Nor is the assertion that Lazkano prohibited the Basque ball matches true. According to testimony of Sebastián Uria, *gudari* of the Loiola battalion, and other witnesses, ball games were played in the *pelota* court on the morning of April 26,[13] and the order to suspend the games in the afternoon was given by the mayor of Gernika, Jose Labauria, as corroborated by Castor Uriarte and Jose Monasterio.[14] Finally, nobody, not even the alleged witnesses mentioned in the Herrán Report, has ever confirmed that there were "pickets of *gudaris* strategically located on the roads of Bilbao."[15] On the contrary, the aforementioned Alberto Onaindia entered Gernika in his vehicle coming from Algorta, through Mungia, by one of the two main access roads to the town, and no one stopped him.[16] The Australian reporter Noel Monks passed through Gernika in his vehicle, coming in this case from the south, from Amorebieta, through the second main access route to Gernika, and left Gernika in the direction of Markina from the third main access road.[17] No one stopped him on route. Joxe Iturria also entered and left Gernika with his truck: "On April 26 I arrived at Gernika from Durango with the truck in the morning. It was market day and there were many people in the village. I parked near the train station. I was there when the bombing began."[18] No witness has ever mentioned any pickets or ever stated that "secondary roads" were used to enter the city.

It is true that Francisco Lazkano was appointed "delegate of the Government in the market of Gernika," but on April 27 – that is, one day after the bombing. In other words, the alleged order to cancel the celebration of the market was issued on April 27, one day after the bombing, and not on the morning of April 26.[19] Castor Uriarte reproduced documentation of this order in his book about the bombing written in 1976 and Talón published his book in 1987.

Other authors have also tried to minimize the number of people in Gernika on the afternoon of April 26. Richthofen, responsible for organizing and executing the bombing, wrote in his diary four days after the event that "the inhabitants were, most of them, out of town at a festival, most of those who stayed left the town from the beginning of the attack. A small part perished in shelters that received impacts."[20] Later, in a letter sent to General Alfredo Kindelán, he added that most of those who stayed in Gernika left the town at the beginning of the bombing, taking refuge on a hill. Obviously, no "festival" in the vicinity of Gernika was ever held, since this area was part of the front line.

This "idea" was passed on to the Non-intervention Committee. Ribbentrop and the two Italian representatives on the committee, Dino Grandi and Guido Crolla, said that the people killed in Gernika, "a city of secondary or tertiary importance,"[21] were not many and that, as a consequence, the case did not deserve special attention, since the number of fatalities was negligible.[22]

To this day, some authors have tried to minimize the number of potential victims in Gernika before the attack. In line with the telegram from the Salamanca General Headquarters to General Sperrle, commander-in-chief of the Condor Legion, of May 7, 1937, which stated that Gernika "had less than 5,000 inhabitants,"[23] James S. Corum states that "Gernika was a small town of 5,000–7,000 inhabitants, and not a 'city' as described by the media of the time."[24] Corum is right; Gernika is not a city, and its population amounted to 5,630 inhabitants according to the census of 1936,[25] although Gonzalo Cárdenas, architect of the General Directorate of Devastated Regions, estimated that Gernika had 6,000 inhabitants,[26] and the plan for the reconstruction of Gernika of the General Directorate of Devastated Regions estimated that the village had 6,234 inhabitants in 1936.[27] In any case, thousands of refugees and war-wounded were added to the number of residents, in addition to those who arrived in the town in search of food on trains arranged by the Basque authorities, all of which supposes a total of between 10,000 and 12,000 people, according to the testimonies of those who travelled to o Gernika on that day.[28] But Corum fails to mention this.

One last reflection on this skein of lies and omissions: Talón does not explain how Lazkano could cancel the market when, according to Olazabal and other witnesses included in the Herrán Report, by virtue of the secret evacuation order there was no longer anyone in Gernika on the afternoon of the 26th. None of these authors have ever claimed that the ball games announced for the 26th were scheduled for the afternoon of that day; specifically, they should have begun a quarter-hour after the bombing began. That is, regardless of whether Jose Labauria decided to cancel the matches, they could never have been held because at mid-afternoon there was nothing left of the ball court.

The direct testimonies of the witnesses of the celebration of the market are numerous and consistent. Civilians did not flee from Gernika, but rather towards Gernika. After the fall of the front in Markina and Lekeitio, these people had abandoned everything they had and went to Gernika, Bermeo, and Mungia, escaping attacks of the rebel aviation along the road that links Eibar and Zornotza, defended by the Basque troops in retreat.

Chapter 4

Gernika has not been bombed: It has been destroyed by fire and gasoline

On the early morning of April 27, Franco issued the order to deny that Gernika or any other city center had been bombed and to denounce the systematic destruction of the cities by the retreating "Reds." General Carlo Bossi immediately transmitted the order to Rome: "Aguirre, head of the Basque Government, today made statements on the radio denouncing the supposed destruction of sacred places carried out by Nationalist aerial bombardments, exhorting the Basque people to the most vigorous resistance. General Franco has arranged an immediate denial, by the same means, denouncing the fierce system of the Reds to burn and destroy all urban centers before retreating. Eibar, occupied by the Nationalists, has been almost completely destroyed by the Reds in flight, with fire and with dynamite."[1]

Both lies (that Gernika was never bombed and that Gernika had been destroyed by the Basques themselves) have their origin in Franco's order, which became the regime's official truth until his death in 1975. Following these instructions to the letter, the propaganda machinery of the insurgent side reproduced these lies throughout the media:

> We want tell the world, very loudly and very clear, a few words about the Guernica fire. Guernica has been destroyed by fire and gasoline. They have set it on fire and the red hordes have turned it into ruins in the criminal service of Aguirre, president of the Basque Republic. The fire occurred yesterday, and Aguirre has launched the infamous lie, because he is a common criminal, attributing to the noble and heroic Air Force of our national Army that crime. It can be proved at any moment that the national Aviation did not fly yesterday because of the fog, neither on

Guernica nor on any other point of the front of Vizcaya. The national Aviation has flown today over Guernica. It has flown and taken photographs of the Guernica fire, which appears almost totally destroyed. Aguirre has felt diabolical and has prepared, in a display of disgusting histrionics, the destruction of Guernica, endorsing it to the adversary and seeking a movement of indignation among the Basques who, defeated and demoralized, can no longer react but in virtue of a great convulsion like this. If the holy tree of Guernica has perished in the hecatomb, it is Aguirre and his people who have killed it. We have already said that our Aviation could not carry out that fire because it did not fly yesterday but, in addition, there are witnesses of the Guernica fire set by the Reds, witnesses of their work with the incendiary torch and the oil. Very soon this town will be in our power. We invite the world to come with us to contemplate its ruins. There it will undoubtedly be proved before foreign journalists that the destruction of Guernica could not be caused by incendiary bombs, that its destruction is the work of those who burned Irun and Eibar, of those who always leave a ghostly Spain behind them. Aguirre has just invented the most tragic and despicable of the farces, imitating those who attributed to us the shooting down of that French airplane in which the president of the International Red Cross was traveling, and the bombing of the British Embassy in Madrid. [. . .]. But in addition to the evidence that has already been provided of the Marxist infamy and that will still be provided, the Spain reconquered by Franco is here, in view of the world: serene, calm, free, happy with the national army, which defeats the enemy and reconstructs his Homeland, while the red hordes assassinate, martyr, burn, destroy and lead chaos everywhere. The Basques and the world should know that Aguirre has burned Guernica. There is no more truth than this, which is the only truth.[2]

Other newspapers reproduced the same news on the front page, but in a condensed form. Such is the case of *Proa*:

We want to say to the world loudly and clearly: Guernica was destroyed by fire and gasoline. The hordes at the service of the criminal Aguirre, president of the Basque Republic, have set it on fire and have turned it into ruins. The fire was caused by them and Aguirre has launched the infamous lie because he is a common criminal who blames the crime on the heroic and noble aviation of our National Army. The national Air

Force did not fly on the day of the fire because of the fog. Yesterday, it was when it flew over Guernica and took photographs of the Guernica fire, which appears almost totally destroyed. Aguirre has felt diabolical and in a disgusting display has prepared the destruction of Guernica to endorse it to the adversary and cause a movement of indignation among the Basques who, tired and demoralized, can no longer react. If the holy tree of Guernica has perished, it is Aguirre and his people who have killed it. We have already said that our aviation could not produce that fire because it did not fly on that day. The Basques and the whole world should know that Aguirre has burned Guernica. There is no more truth than this, which is the only truth.[3]

Radio Vitoria, Radio Salamanca, and other regime radio stations read the texts reproduced by the press, with some minor variations. Radio Salamanca's message includes, despite its brevity, no fewer than fifteen falsehoods:

This is not the first time that Aguirre, boss of the Basque Republic, has lied. Aguirre said today that the foreign aviation in the service of national Spain has bombarded Guernica and burned it to hurt the Basques in the depths of their feelings. Aguirre lies, he lies; he knows it well. In the first place, there is no German or foreign aviation in National Spain. There is Spanish aviation, noble and heroic Spanish aviation, which must fight continuously with the red aircraft, which are Russian and French and flown by foreign pilots. Second, we have not set Guernica on fire. Franco's Spain does not burn. The incendiary torch is a monopoly of those who set Irun on fire, who burned down Eibar, and who tried to burn alive the defenders of the Alcazar de Toledo. If we did not know that Aguirre knows that he is lying, as he is as a common criminal, we would remind him that among those who fight in the Vizcayan front next to the 'Gudaris' there are Asturian miners, professionals in destruction by flame and gasoline, and the barbaric dynamite of the Marxist violence with whose collaboration Aguirre has tried to remain a little king.[4]

And the presenter ended up saying: "Franco's army does not burn. The Basque Country knows that we respect and will respect its traditions. Franco's Spain does not burn."[5] This final statement adds three more lies to the previous fifteen. In the broadcasts of April 29 and 30,

Radio Verdad repeated: "It is confirmed that the government has set Guernica on fire, as they did with Eibar and Marquina."[6]

Films also echoed denial of the bombing. The director of the National Delegation of Press and Propaganda of Falange, Dionisio Ridruejo, produced a film with the title *Frente de Vizcaya y 18 de Julio*, which also referred to the burning of the city: "The Jewish and Masonic press of the world and the plaintive hypocrites of Valencia tore their clothes before the Caudillo whose clean name, like our heaven, they tried to stain with the bullet of their slanderous information. The camera, which cannot lie, shows very clearly that such great destruction was nothing but the work of arsonists and dynamiters."[7]

After the capture of Gernika on April 29, the official Francoist report stated that "the indignation of the troops for such barbarous destruction increases their spirit to free the Basque people from their true executioners."[8]

General Gonzalo Queipo de Llano was one of the first propagators of this version of the facts on Radio Sevilla. During an interview for a British newspaper, the *Daily Express*, and following Franco's guidelines, Queipo stated on April 29 that Gernika had not been bombed because the rebel planes had not been able to fly due to bad weather. When the reporter asked him how he could explain that international reporters such as Noel Monks had collected unexploded bombs with German inscriptions on them, he replied that many people had been bought with stolen gold from Spanish banks and related things they had not seen and even offered objects brought from other places in support of their accusations. Queipo underlined that Gernika was not a military target and the city deserved the respect of the Nationalists.[9]

When questioned about why the Basques wanted to destroy their own town and kill their own people, Queipo answered that Spanish Marxism was something unique, run by a number of men who lived on others to support them and was composed of masses of illiterate people whose instincts, corralled by their leaders and their natural inclination to pillage, led them to commit the most horrible crimes. According to Queipo, Republicans killed men, women, and even children by the most horrible means, including burning churches and destroying archives and works of art of incalculable value; Queipo ends by arguing that, in short, the great and civilized English spirit would not understand these things, so they were not to be detailed.[10] Finally, asked if he believed that the Basques themselves blew up their own city by throwing bombs, Queipo blatantly replied that if Gernika had been destroyed, it had been destroyed by the Reds.[11]

The Germans also followed Franco's order and disseminated through institutional channels and the press the idea that Gernika had not been bombed but rather reduced to ashes by the Basques themselves. A report signed in Berlin on April 29, read: "The destruction of Guernica must not have been, as was communicated concordantly, carried out by national aircraft. Instead, it would have been, according to the express communication from the White Headquarters, set on fire by the Reds themselves. It would not have been impossible the use of airplanes that mentioned day [of April 26] given the weather conditions."[12] A second report restated the same version of events but emphasized the credibility of the information received from the Nationalist Headquarters: "Faced with the reports that call attention to the destruction of Guernica, and to the press releases that display fantastic points of view – a correspondent of the Reuters news agency suggested that he counted [saw] Junkers Ju 52 heavy bombers, Heinkel 111 light bombers , and Heinkel 51 fighters during the air attack – the military report issued in Salamanca again indicates in this regard that the city was victim of the fire set by the Bolsheviks when the national troops were still about 15 kilometers from Guernica."[13] The Situation Report No. 252 of April 28, drafted by the Information Service of the High Command of the German Navy, stated that the town was set on fire by the Reds as a "propaganda maneuver [in order to] discredit national Spain."[14]

All pilots involved in the bombing were ordered to maintain silence. Lieutenant Hans von Beust, commander of the second K/88 bombing squadron of Junkers Ju 52 that bombed Gernika, said that "the Legion's command had ordered the action under the supervision of the Spanish command, or at their request [. . .]. We, the crews of the K/88 [of Junkers Ju 52], were already encouraged the same day, when the wave of propaganda was already starting, and the results of the reconnaissance confirmed a great level of destruction, not to mention the attack and make denial of it where appropriate."[15]

The German ambassador in Salamanca immediately sent instructions to the Ministry of Foreign Affairs in Berlin:

> The press office of the national government has [issued] on April 29 and 30 detailed reports [. . .] about the fire of Guernica, which were handed over to representatives of the foreign press, rejecting with most intensity

as lies and slander, the communiqué of the Basque Government on the alleged destruction of the city by German aviators. [. . .] I attach the translation of some nuclear passages of the denial of April 29: 'Guernica has been destroyed by fire and gasoline. The red hordes have burned and reduced it to rubble in the criminal service of Aguirre, the President of the Basque Republic. Aguirre has engineered the destruction of Guernica with the demonic intention of accusing the enemy of it and provoking a general indignation among the Basques, already defeated and demoralized.[16]

Consequently, as the correspondent of *Les Temps* observed, "following the order" the German press described in block type and with identical prose "the legend of Guernica" as a "Bolshevik lie destined to distract attention" from other bloody incidents perpetrated by the Republicans during the war.[17] The *Berliner Lokal-Anzeiger*, one of the most widely circulated newspapers in Germany, reported that the fire in Gernika had been provoked by the retreating "Bolsheviks" themselves and added: "The story of German aircraft is a legend, since no air attack has taken place against Gernika."[18] The *Berliner Tageblatt* published an article under the headline "Scary Tales to Divert Attention," referring to the "clumsy maneuvers of the Bolsheviks."[19] The *Völkischer Beobachter* described the statements of the Lehendakari Agirre as "brazen Bolshevik lies exceeding all limits of human impudence as a pretext to attack totally disinterested states."[20] The *Börsen-Zeitung* denounced the "vile campaign of agitation directed by the English leftist newspapers not only against General Franco, but also directly against Germany in an attempt to inflame world public opinion in favor of *the poor Basque people*."[21] Following the Francoist propoganda, the *Berliner Illustrierte Nachtausgabe* reported that bad weather prevented the planes from flying on April 26.[22]

The Italian press operated the same way and published the same material, sometimes literal translations of the Francoist version. For example, Radio Milan transmitted that the Republicans practiced a scorched earth strategy, but, given that Irun was a locality unknown to the Italian public, they preferred to refer to Lekeitio, which was occupied on April 29 by Italian units at the command of the General Sandro Piazzoni and that, therefore, the following was being cited in the headlines of a large number of Italian newspapers: "From the beginning of the operations the towns through which the Marxists pass are left sunken in misery or in flames. Yesterday it was Eibar, Lequeitio; today Guernica, the holy city. Captured prisoners confirm that the fires were intentionally provoked. The joy of the liberated populations is enormous."[23]

However, the quantity and quality of the news about the bombing as well as the material evidence of it was so overwhelming that the story that Gernika had not been bombed simply did not take hold. The free world's press quickly and broadly disseminated testimonies of eye-witnesses to the bombing and the articles written by prestigious international reporters such as Noel Monks, George Steer, Mathieu Corman, Christopher Home, Scott Watson, and Martin Arrisbaya to a point that it was simply impossible to maintain the propaganda version. As the *London Times* reported, "Salamanca's refusal to completely ignore the destruction of Guernica did not created the slightest astonishment in London, since the bombing of Durango had been also denied in spite of the presence of eyewitnesses."[24] On the other hand, the German and Italian media leaked news of the bombing. Despite the official denial and the constant press articles about the destruction of Gernika by fire and gasoline, the *Frankfurter Zeitung* published an article on "modern warfare," detailing the use of aircraft and firebombs in Gernika.[25]

Robert Mackinnon Wood, head of the Department of Aerodynamic Investigations of the British Navy, was in the Basque Country between May 23 and 28 investigating the nationality of the airplanes operating in Bizkaia. He showed a total of fifty photographs to the survivors of the bombing of Gernika in order to identify the planes that took part in the bombing. He also interviewed the German pilot Hans J. Wandel (who had piloted a Heinkel He 51 over Gernika together with Friedrich Franz Cramon[26]) and personally saw German planes operating in the front that without any doubt he identified as Heinkel He 111 bombers and Heinkel He 51 fighters, all which he noted in his report, to which logically the British authorities had access.[27]

At the beginning of May 1937, when the controversy about the bombing was in full eruption and the matter was being discussed, among many other forums, in the British Parliament, in the U.S. Congress, within the Non-intervention Committee, and in the Assembly of the League of Nations, it was obvious that the version that Gernika had been "destroyed by the incendiary torch" could only be maintained within the borders of the regime, where all media were censored and there was a monopoly on the "official truth."

However, beyond these borders it was necessary to use an alternative version, "a more credible official truth." The Duke of Alba wrote to Franco in May 1937 from London asking for a "scientific" report on the destruction of Gernika, including professional statements.[28] This is the origin of the Herrán Report, an allegedly scientific report written under Francoist supervision that admitted that a "minor" bombing had occurred and concluded that the main destruction of the city was due to a fire.

But, even though the regime allowed this version of the event to be leaked abroad, Franco never retracted nor accepted that Gernika had been bombed, and this was the official version maintained by the dictatorship for forty years. Although few authors have defended the hypothesis of the fire of Gernika after 1945, Jeffrey Hart, in an article published in the *National Review* on January 5, 1973, about "The Great Guernica Fraud," repeated some of the ideas expressed by the Falangist propaganda and expressed the view that Gernika was indeed a legitimate military objective, because "there are eight roads there," and added that these objectives were not in town, so the planes repeatedly bombarded the military targets while the city center was never bombed, but rather destroyed by the fire.[29]

Chapter 5

Gernika was bombed, but the destruction was mainly due to the fire

Franco's order to lie engendered the outright denial that Gernika had been bombed. The regime, especially General Queipo de Llano and Luis Bolín, spread this version of the facts by all means possible. However, a blatant denial was impossible to maintain. The Francoist version of what took place on the day lacked credibility and was subject to the testimonies and material evidence collected in Gernika by international reporters. Moreover, while the versions of Franco's propaganda and diplomacy began to diversify to the point of incoherence, the information provided by reporters, observers, and foreign diplomats who visited Gernika, being perfectly testable, presented a consistent and verifiable body of evidence.

This explains why, while Franco's version of the events was reproduced without much variation in Nazi Germany, fascist Italy, and Oliveira Salazar's Portugal, it barely reverberated in the French Republic and had almost no impact on the British and American press. The reports by international reporters who witnessed the destruction of the town spread around the world because news of the bombing generated unprecedented panic and also because the credibility of Noel Monks, George Steer, Mathieu Corman, Christopher Holme, and Scott Watson was beyond reproach. The manifestly incongruous versions of General Queipo de Llano, Luis Bolín, Alfonso Merry del Val, and the Marquis of Moral simply did not convince the reading public.

News of the bombing quickly spread throughout the world and became front-page news in many newspapers in European and American democracies. In the absence of a quantitative study of the impact of the news in the United Kingdom or, by extension, in Western Europe, we can note that more than 7,000 articles about the bombing were published in the United States between April 27 and July 4, 1937. Forty of the 63 articles on the bombing published by the *New York Times* (63 percent) in this period emphasized the fact that the town was totally destroyed, and 80 percent of the articles registered on April 27 in American newspapers about the bombing were published on the first page.[1]

Faced with this media impact, Franco's order barely reached a few right-wing newspapers in a handful of democratic countries. The truth prevailed, and the Gernika version of the fire did not convince the public internationally.

After initial international reactions to the bombing, Lehendakari Agirre proposed that the Non-intervention Committee or a neutral agency conduct an unbiased investigation on the destruction of Gernika.[2] Pablo Azcarate, ambassador of the Spanish Republic in London, and the Spanish delegate to the League of Nations Julio Álvarez del Vayo, immediately seconded the proposal, which was also well received by the Labor opposition in the House of Commons in the UK, as well as among some American senators and congressmen.

Lieutenant Knauer, commander of the first Junkers Ju 52 K/88 squadron that bombed Gernika, recalled "that General Sperrle received a proposal from the London ambassador von Ribbentrop, about whether a combined international commission could go to Guernica, in order to convince [the public] that the German bombs had never produced the main destruction. The Condor Legion sent bomb experts to Guernica to clean all the remains of bomb fins, unexploded grenades, etc. After this, Ambassador Ribbentrop received the news that a commission could go to Guernica at any time."[3] However, the fact is that when on May 8, 1937, General Sperrle, Commander-in-Chief of the Condor Legion, consulted Franco about the possibility of taking an international commission to Gernika to decide if the town had been bombed or burned, he "uttered a categorical no," although by early May most of the evidence had already been removed or destroyed.[4]

Before Franco's refusal, both Ribbentrop and Dino Grandi, German and Italian delegates at the Non-intervention Committee, received from their respective administrations the order to oppose any investigation into the facts.[5] As a result, they denied that Gernika had been bombed and threatened to abandon the system of non-intervention if the representatives of the rest of the member states continued to press for the organization of this investigative commission. Moreover, in an exercise of cynicism, Ribbentrop pointed out that in May 1935 Hitler had already made public his categorical and unconditional repudiation of aerial bombings and had expressed the need to draw up an international convention to regulate air warfare.

However, the circumstances required a change of direction in the regime's propaganda campaign. It was necessary to diversify the lie and make it more flexible so that the initial denial gave way to the first versions of the reductionist literature, which tended to accept that there had been a bombing but altered its nature and minimized its impact and consequences. In this way, maintaining the official version, within the borders of the dictatorship, that Gernika had been destroyed by fire and gasoline, the Francoist regime's propaganda machinery spread abroad the idea that indeed a "light bombardment" had taken place and had been exploited by Basque forces to burn down the village and blame the coup plotters for it. At the same time, Frederick-Ramón de Bertodano, Marqués del Moral, coordinator of the pro-Franco propaganda office in London in 1937, recommended that Franco stop Luis Bolín, one of the most active journalists, from spreading the news of the Gernika fire. Just three weeks after the bombing, on May 14, Bolín was discharged, and Pablo Merry de Val was named "special envoy" of the coup government to the United Kingdom, the Nordic countries, and the United States.

In order to silence the opinions expressed in the British media, and with the intention of imbuing the Francoist version of the facts, a "scientific" character, the road engineer Vicente Machimbarrena, was ordered to prepare a report: "The chief of General Staff, current General [Juan] Vigón and Minister of the Air, entrusted me with the writing of a report, together with the mining engineer Miláns del Bosch, to find out the causes of the destruction of the town of Guernica, where we arrived a few hours after being taken by the National Army."[6] And, as Machimbarrena related, in a matter of a few hours, on their way through Eibar, they could confirm that Eibar had been "destroyed by 80% as a result of fire produced by flammable materials. We verified, then, that in those days, expert dynamiters and arsonists accompanied the enemy hordes to carry out systematically their destructive work when leaving the places we occupied."[7]

Having confirmed this fact in record time when entering Gernika, or even earlier, as they passed through Errenteria, both engineers observed the first material signs of the fire: "When entering Guernica through the Renteria neighborhood and before passing the bridge that exists on the estuary, we observed, on the left side, that a group of houses had disappeared by the fire, not yet completely extinguished."[8] However, unlike the versions published in the press on previous days, the authors of this report expressed that they had seen clearly the effects of a light aerial bombing.[9] The conclusion, after "about two hours" of conscientious examination, was therefore that Gernika had been lightly bombed, without any serious damage being found, but the real destruction of the village was due to the fire: "We went through different streets of the city and in all of them the traces of a systematic fire are obvious. The houses, in fact, have disappeared due to the collapse of roofs and floors, but some of them [partial canvases of the façades] still remain that, in the event that the ruin had been produced by violent explosions of bombs, would not have stayed in that state. As a detail that proves this statement, we note that some walls of façades fell to the ground while maintaining the orderly succession of the brick courses, which would have been impossible in case of an explosion."[10]

Against hard evidence and without regard to the truth, both authors stated that on Monday, April 26, rebel aviation flew over Gernika "throwing several projectiles on military targets, such as the Institute and two or three convents on the periphery, used by the militiamen as barracks."[11] In reality, as the aerial photographs taken after the bombing show, the convents on the outskirts of Gernika were never attacked. Machimbarrena and Miláns del Bosch concluded that the German planes had dropped between six or eight bombs in total:

> However, on our journey, we have seen funnels – in number of six or eight – of different depth and extent, caused by aviation bombs, with the peculiarity that several coincide with the sewer line. The deepest we saw was one in the entrance crossing, another in the street transverse to it, called January 8, and, exceptionally, one in the upper part of the city, which is the only one that has not been affected much. We also verified that at least one of them coincided with the sewer line. However, both at this point and in general throughout the whole city, you cannot ascertain, due to the state in which it is, all covered by huge debris shawls, whether mines or simple charges of dynamite had been previously placed in the sewers.[12]

Finally, referring to bombs with inscriptions in German that had been found in the village and sent to the United Kingdom by British reporters, the authors added that "throughout our tour by the destroyed city neither we nor any of the many people with whom we spoke found any piece of shrapnel."[13]

Basing their story on the testimony of a single witness "of quality and solvency," Machimbarrena and Miláns del Bosch were the first to add that the actions of local firemen had been deficient and that the fire could have been extinguished with a few buckets of water:

> Some of us were told that the first isolated sources of fire could easily be extinguished, but that absolutely nothing was done to achieve this. What's more, a reliable witness assured us that he saw at nightfall on the 26th some small fires on one street that, according to his own words, 'could have been extinguished with a few buckets of water' and that the most pious thing that can be thought is that nothing was done, since the next morning he saw, with surprise, that the fire had destroyed almost all the buildings in town. It follows from the foregoing that the almost complete destruction of Guernica, which exceeds that of Irun and Eibar, could not have been caused by the bombing of a squadron of planes during a single afternoon.[14]

Machimbarrena and Miláns del Bosch's report was delivered to Colonel Juan Vigón on May 1, 1937, in Gasteiz. However, given its brevity and the fact that it was written in Spanish, the Duke of Alba advised a second, longer report be written and published as a book in English to be distributed in the United Kingdom in response to press articles on the subject. The result is the report entitled *Guernica: Being the official report of a commission appointed by the Spanish National Government to investigate the causes of the destruction of Guernica on April 26–28, 1937.* Drafted by Estanislao Herrán, Tomás Pereda, José Usera, and Joaquín García Tuñón, it is known as the Herrán Report. The authors met in Gernika on August 9, and signed the report in Burgos in September. The text was translated into English and published and distributed in the United Kingdom by Eyre & Spottiswoode in 1938. The authors listed fourteen conclusions, all of which are false.

Obviously, the first conclusion of the Herrán Report was that "Guernica was destroyed by fire."[15] The fourth to tenth observations of the report describe the alternative truth of the aforementioned authors

and, by extension, the official truth of the regime outside the borders of
its territory:

> (iv) At four o'clock on the afternoon of the 26th April the few inhabitants
> who remained in Guernica observed the appearance of certain aero-
> planes. They thereupon took refuge in the shelters and saw nothing of
> what took place in the town up to half-past seven in the evening, at which
> hour they ventured forth. (v) For three hours and a half, and throughout
> the following night, the inhabitants of Guernica listened to heavy explo-
> sions which took place within the town. (vi) Near the network of
> highways to the east of Guernica several aerial bombs fell. It appeared
> that the object of these bombs was to cut the communications. (vii) No
> signs are visible of the explosion of any aerial bombs within the town.
> (viii) The explosions heard within the town by the inhabitants of
> Guernica were the result of dynamite detonated in the sewers and in
> other parts of the town, in accordance with the Basque Government's
> prearranged plan. (ix) At eight o'clock on the night of the 26th April,
> when the townsfolk left the shelters, a certain number of houses in
> Guernica began to burn. It would have been an easy matter to have put
> out these fires and to repair the damage caused up to that time. After
> the above-mentioned hour no aeroplanes flew over Guernica, nor in its
> neighbourhood, up to the time our soldiers entered. The destruction of
> Guernica, therefore, cannot be attributed to German planes. (x) From
> this hour onwards (eight o'clock in the evening of the 26th April) the
> inhabitants were able to see what was taking place in the town. The Red
> militiamen not only took no steps to check the conflagration, but they
> prevented the townsfolk from taking steps to that end. For three succes-
> sive days these militiamen continued to set fires alight and to help them
> to spread; and some of this work was continued later, even after, our
> troops had entered Guernica.[16]

The conclusion of all the above is that "it can safely be affirmed that
the greater part of this damage was caused by fire, as is shown by the
smoke-stains observable in the lintels of the doors and windows of the
lower floors, by the carbonised wooden beams, by the window frames
which have been reduced to ashes, by the walls or remains thereof which
have remained upright in a manner which could not have occurred if any
nearby explosion had caused them to rock, by the iron beams twisted by
the heat of the fire, by the transmission machinery of the little work-

shops also twisted by the same cause, and by the fallen walls. Very few indeed are the houses destroyed by the action of explosives."[17] The authors omitted the observations of Colonel Joachim von Richthofen,[18] who wrote that the walls remain standing after a bombardment with incendiaries and explosives with delayed fuse, which was the case in Gernika and Eibar: "Italian breaker bombs of 100 kilos were mainly used. In cases where they hit the target, these projectiles crossed four floors and reached the basement [of the building]. The funnels could not be examined when filled with rubble. The walls did not collapse."[19]

The reporters omitted the launching of incendiary bombs and conceived the idea that expert dynamiters placed charges on the public sewer network. That is, they lied by action and omission and avoided describing how the bombing took place. As Joachim von Richthofen himself expressed in his diary and in the report he wrote, based on his own observations in May 1938, the first bombers destroyed the town's water pipes and, subsequently, dropped explosive bombs on the city center to destroy the buildings. Finally, they launched incendiaries whose flammable material penetrated the wooden interior of the structures, knocking them down by fire: "The 250-kilo bombs demolished a good number of houses and destroyed the water pipes. The incendiary bombs now had time to deploy their full effectiveness. The houses were built with tile roofs, wooden galleries, and latticework of the same material, so they were completely destroyed."[20] Obviously, launching approximately 6,000 incendiary bombs with the potential to raise temperatures to more than $1,500°$ C in an area of less than one square kilometer caused an uncontrollable fire. This, together with the destruction of the water pumping system, explains the fatal spread of fire.

To endorse the Francoist version of the events, the report included the testimony of people like Pedro Olivárez, who testified before the Herrán Commission "[t]hat he was in that town on the 26th of April last, and that about four o'clock in the afternoon there appeared over Guernica a three-engined aeroplane. This was attacked by an anti-aircraft gun, *after which* [in italics in the original text] it dropped some seven bombs, which fell near the Renteria bridge and the Convent of La Merced."[21] All this is false; the participation of between 59 and 62 aircraft over Gernika is documented, and there was no anti-aircraft defense system in town. However, through this version the authors of the report reduced the number of aircraft and stressed that this first aircraft bombed Gernika only after it was attacked.

All witnesses collected by the Herrán Commission described, as if repeating a catchphrase, the same reality: that the bombers focused their attacks on targets on the outskirts of Gernika, suggesting that it was a strategic bombing, and that the ruin of the city center was due solely to the destructive action organized by the Basque government. Most of the informants examined by the Herrán Commission stated that a few aircraft dropped some explosive (and non-incendiary) bombs on the suburbs of Gernika between 3:30 and 8:00 in the afternoon but that the cause of the destruction was the fire that the firemen simply did not want to put out. Such is the case of Luis Gomez, 37 years of age, who declared "[t]hat the first lot of bombs fell in the neighbourhood of the station, about 500 metres from the centre of the town, and that the largest fell towards the bridge and cross-roads known as Renteria, where the Ajanguiz, Arrazua and Arteaga roads meet. He could not see whether these aeroplanes dropped incendiary bombs."[22]

The corollary of all the above was therefore that

on the Basque Government decreeing the evacuation of Guernica, a conflagration broke out in the town, which was aided and abetted in three distinct manners by the guards, the '*ertzañas*' [Basque police] and the militiamen under their command, namely by omitting to extinguish it, by forbidding its extinction, and by aiding its extension. Neither the firemen nor the armed men who occupied the town took any steps to put it out; the townsfolk who by all means in their power sought to avert the catastrophe were not permitted so to do. The firemen and their comrades would not take any steps even when a reward was offered. During those hours the casual spectator would only have seen in Guernica disorder and desolation; but closer observation would have detected careful organisation. Each explosion occurred at the pre-arranged moment, each fire was set alight by the agent previously designated and at the precise moment when those who had planned it were at their respective posts and ran no risk. For the others – what did it matter! They were of no importance as likely as not they were aged men, women and children, whose corpses would serve admirably for the purpose of propaganda against the Army of Liberation.[23]

The editors of the Herrán report insisted that there were clear signs of explosions produced by dynamite charges placed strategically by the Basques, who then proceeded to cover the holes caused by the dynamite from April 27 to 28, before entry of the rebel troops into the village. Since much of the sewage system was intact, they had to affirm that, although it had been blown up, the dynamiters subsequently restored the holes produced by the explosions!:

> All these craters are outside the town of Guernica, close to the bridge and to the cluster of roads which run from its eastern side leading from Lequeitio, Marquina and Durango. In the interior of the town the Commission was unable to find any trace of a crater, although, had any existed, there are numerous gardens and public squares where they would still have remained as clearly visible as they are in the fields on the eastern side, where is the cluster of roads mentioned. On the other hand, inside the town zone may be seen signs of great explosions on the roads, streets, public squares and boulevards. These explosions must have been very powerful and destructive; but the holes which they left in the ground have been filled in, the pavement repaired, and only by close observation of this paving can the recent and imperfect repairs be noticed as a large patch in the road surface. [. . .] Dynamite cartridges, with detonators and fuses which would explode the dynamite could easily be so introduced and reproduce exactly the marks left by the explosions within the urban area of Guernica. This procedure could be easily carried out by anybody.[24]

One of the major drawbacks of the official Francoist version was that witnesses to the bombing had obtained material evidence of the raid in the town. Such is the case of Monks and Steer, who took from the ruins unexploded incendiary bombs whose carcasses were inscribed with the place and date of manufacture and an eagle, symbol of the Luftwaffe. Other bombs were marked with the inscription "Rome", providing evidence that the Italian airplanes had also dropped incendiary bombs. In order to counteract this material evidence, the "eyewitnesses" of the Herrán Report asserted that the Basque police had placed incendiary bombs among the ruins to blame the Francoist army for everything:

> Among the ruins have been found various stabilisers belonging to incendiary aerial bombs, and these have been used as an argument for imputing the origin of the fire to such a cause. But the flaw in this argument is that, at eight o'clock on the night of 26th April, when the townsfolk left the shelters and those who had gone into the country

returned, only a few houses were burning and the fire could have been got under control. The fire began when the townsfolk had taken refuge in the shelters owing to fear of the explosions, so that no one saw how it commenced, and it has been impossible to clear up the question of the origin of the above-mentioned stabilisers. At any rate, they were not stamped with the German eagle, nor with the word 'Rome', as alleged by the Red propaganda. It is, indeed, only reasonable to suppose that those who refused to allow the fire to be extinguished had in fact started it. Especially when they had previously blazoned it abroad that 'if the Fascists capture the town from us, they will find nothing but a heap of ashes.' Again, a conflagration caused from the air always begins from the top downwards, and there are none such in Guernica.[25]

Plácido Iturbe, a 40-year-old Talleres de Guernica worker, testified before the Herrán commission that fire bombs were produced in the factory, implying that these were the ones used to burn Gernika: "That the witness knows that incendiary bombs were manufactured in the above-mentioned workshops, and that the distinctive features of the stabilisers of these bombs were similar to those of the stabilisers found after the bombing of Guernica which took place on the 26th April last. That he saw some of these in nearby market-gardens, but that he did not keep any."[26] Moreover, the Herrán report included a second testimony from this same witness who explained "that after having made a declaration yesterday he went to the spot where he found the stabilisers which had been used during the bombing on the 26th April last, to see if he could find another one. And he found two stabilisers calcined [oxidized], with spindles, belonging to the incendiary bombs. He [showed] an incendiary bomb made in the Talleres de Guernica (Guernica workshops), which he found in those workshops where he is employed."[27]

The authors of the report also underlined the fact that explosions were heard throughout the night in Gernika. These were explosive bombs that simply exploded not when they fell but later on due to high temperatures, something common in aerial bombardment. Obviating this fact and without any material evidence to confirm it, the signatories of the report assured that

> a part from all that has already been said, it is well to take note of one singular fact, and that is that all the witnesses, without exception, agree in stating that after leaving the shelters and throughout the night of the

26th to the 27th they noticed numerous explosions within the town bounds; some of these were of great intensity, such as those which they noticed when they were hidden in the shelters and which they had attributed to aerial bombs. None of the witnesses even thought of suggesting that these nocturnal explosions were the result of aerial bombs, as the night was dark, and no aeroplanes could have ventured a flight among the mountains at that hour with any hope of success, nor could they have managed to drop their projectiles on any particular objectives; such systematic destruction could only have been wrought by dynamiters within the town, and it is significant that these explosions continued with increasing frequency and intensity from eleven o'clock all through the night; that is to say, from the time that the Basque Government motor-cars reached Guernica.[28]

The Herrán Report emphasized the finding of gasoline in Gernika: "On the boarded floor of the church of San Juan the traces of burning petrol can still be seen. The scorched edges of these holes prove beyond doubt their origin, as do those which appear on the floor of the stage of the cinema shown in plate 14 [photographs included in the report]. There also it is plain that the petrol was thrown about on both sides and lighted. The projection-room has also been burnt out inside, but outside it is intact, a fact which would indeed be strange did one exclude the suggestion of intention. Before the projectionroom was set on fire it was looted, nothing remaining in it except worthless effects."[29] However, the authors were careful to note that there was a gas station next to the church of San Juan, which obviously explains the existence of fuel drums. They even took photographs of the drums, included on page 83 of the report, as evidence of the fire in the village.

Both Richthofen and Jaenecke, as well as some of the pilots who participated in the attack on Gernika, insisted on this theory, proposed for the first time by Machimbarrena and Miláns del Bosch and later reproduced and expanded in the Herrán Report with its emphasis on the light bombing and subsequent fire of the town. Hans von Beust, head of the second K/88 bomber squad of Junkers Ju 52 that bombed Gernika, said, "I still have it clear before my eyes the image that was offered to me during the flyby. There is evidence that the destructions that caused the bombing was considerable. I do not think the Reds subsequently destroyed it even more."[30] Lieutenant Karl von Knauer, head of the first K/88 Junkers Ju 52 squad that bombarded Gernika, decided to lie differently and generated a new version of the events. According to him, although the objective of the bombing was the bridge, because of "a lateral wind of the NE [north-east]" and a certain "deviation of the series of bombs towards the west," "the eastern edge of the town" was "partially" affected by the bombs[31] where the Reds had stored large amounts of dynamite that exploded when bombed. And he added, deliberately omitting any reference to the launching of 250-kilogram bombs and thousands of incendiaries, that "the effects of our 50 kilos bombs could had never been so violent. As I can tell [conversation of my interpreter with natives of the town]), the so-called 'dynamiters' had large deposits of explosives in town, whose explosion was caused either by our attack, or a later one. And only in this way could the enormous destruction have been undertaken, and that is the only way to explain it. I reported this in detail to Lieutenant Colonel von Richthofen and also to my immediate superior, Commander [Robert] Fuchs."[32]

The *Report on the Situation of the Basque Provinces under the Red-Separatist Domain*, published in 1938 by Manuel Ferrandis, Ricardo Magdaleno, and Francisco Antón, professors of the University of Valladolid, took some ideas about the bombing of and subsequent fire in Gernika from the Herrán Report. By virtue of this report, Gernika was a legitimate military target, and the Francoist army "destroyed military targets, broke up concentrations of troops, drove the enemy away, and respected 'with loving care' everything that was not of military interest in Gernika. But this was not what suited the premeditated propaganda that the separatist leaders thought to take abroad and, in order to enjoy the "disguise of victims," they dedicated themselves to the task of dynamiting the village "[. . .] and then new fires sprout[ed] in the city, mysterious detonations were heard, intact houses disappeared after two days of the war action and, for a week, from the heights of Rigoitia, the fugitive militiamen insistently shelled the Church and the House of Meetings that then received cannon impacts, fortunately scarce, that are today a good example of the 'love' with which those who allegedly loved her so much said goodbye."[33] And the report concluded "with this categorical affirmation that no one can deny":

> Those same days when they were about to destroy the historic and sentimental center of Guernica, how many hypocritical lamentations did they throw at the world? They had transformed it into a warlike center

and complained that war came to it; they had been its executioners and they hurried to show themselves as victims before the truth emerged. But the truth always arrives and, when verified by our documented testimony, annuls what the Red propaganda affirmed. There is no premeditated and useless destruction, however insignificant, that can be attributed to the glorious forces of the National Army.[34]

This version of events – that after a light bombing, locals proceeded to burn the village – has been one of the most widespread lies about Gernika. One of the later authors repeating this idea was Brian Crozier, who published a brief note in the London *Times* in July 1969 in which he stated that there was, in fact, a small nationalist air raid, in which the targets were the railway station and a weapons factory. According to the author, some German bombs may have also fallen in the city, but the massive destruction was caused by the systematic dynamiting of a neighborhood of Gernika, and only of one neighborhood.[35] The note was reproduced in the *Daily Telegraph* in which Crozier asserted that the bombing of Gernika was a myth and that most of the destruction was in fact caused by retreating Republican dynamite squads. The author ended by expressing that "the truth is great and must prevail."[36]

De la Cierva cited the testimony of Lieutenant Colonel José Martínez Esparza, head of one of the groups of the Fourth Brigade that entered Gernika on April 29. An article written De la Cierva under the title "Memories of the Occupation of Guernica" and published in the Army magazine in July 1949 states verbatim that "the stoves for the dynamite were clearly visible, some placed on the upper floors of the buildings."[37] De la Cierva asserted that "in virtue of the category of the witness the testimony is conclusive."[38] Crozier also referred to the destruction of "a single neighborhood" of Gernika, but photographs of the bombing show that the destruction was absolute, affecting 99 percent of all the buildings in the town. Like other authors who stressed the strategic value of Gernika, Crozier avoided clarifying to the reader that neither the railway station nor the arms factories were destroyed.

Contemporary revisionist historiography continues to legitimize the Herrán Report, and some authors make use of it as a historical source even though it is obviously not a scientific study or a document that meets the most elementary criteria of verisimilitude. Jaime del Burgo also emphasized that Gernika was set afire, stating that "the testimony of the company of sappers from Pamplona, which shortly after carried out the work of clearing, revealed without any doubt traces of dynamite charges placed after the bombing, which ended at seven thirty in the afternoon."[39] Jesús Salas, in the three editions of his book about the bombing, the last of which was released in 2012, repeated the version of the Herrán Report almost word for word: "Firefighters from Bilbao were alerted very late, did not arrive until after 10 o'clock at night and went back at three o'clock in the morning without adopting adequate measures taking into consideration the magnitude of the fire."[40] The author then affirmed, based solely on testimonies provided by the Herrán Report, that "they brought three pumps to kill the fire and they had a plentiful of hoses and all the water of the Mundaca estuary."[41] Salas even cited the witness Pedro Olivares, stating that "Pedro Olivares Arana stopped pouring water on his house, according to him because the firemen received a higher order to remove the water pumps. This happened before the foreign correspondents, who had arrived in Guernica at eleven o'clock at night, returned to Bilbao, because Olivares had a short conversation with them in the Asilo Calzada Street."[42] And he concluded by saying that "the attitude of the firemen and the militiamen was described as passive by eight of the 22 witnesses of the Herran report (namely, Obieta, Madariaga, Gomeza, Blanco, Pardo, Olazabal, Iturriarte, and Olivares) and seven others gave even tougher qualifications, while the remaining seven did not say anything on this particular."[43]

Under the offensive epigraph "Born to burn," Vicente Talón also expressed in 1987 the idea that the destruction of the town was mainly caused not by the bombing itself but rather by the deficient work of the fire services: "Towards three in the morning, very few hours after its appearance, the firemen broke up their camp and hurried back to Bilbao. It is not that they were called for any important mission, but with the front broken and with enemy troops in advance, the fear of being isolated provoked anguishing cramps in their bellies and swiftness in their feet. Guernica, an immense brazier, was thus left to her own efforts, to her own ability to survive."[44] The author, who made use of the Herrán Report as a historical source, concluded that "the passivity or opposition of the firefighters and militiamen to extinguish the flames poses some interest. This is a dark episode, given the fact that during my research in Guernica I found those who complained that their houses burned for nothing, because nobody helped them to kill the fire."[45] According to Talón, most of the people he interviewed "spoke of passivity and incompetence," although no one suggested that the Basque firemen were at any point trying to avoid or hinder the fight against the fire. Nonetheless, the author continued, the Herrán Report included the testimonies of several victims who "also expressed this last possibility."[46] And he quoted Pedro Olivares and the rest of the seven witnesses mentioned by Salas.

And this version, based on a report that lacks legitimacy, drafted on behalf of the regime that ordered the execution of the bombing and short of documentation that endorses its findings, continues to circulate. In March 2017, Professor Jorge Vilches, of the Universidad Complutense of Madrid, repeated that when the British reporter George Steer arrived in Gernika "everything was in flames, partly because of the inefficiency of the firemen."[47] Moreover, Vilches, who based his version on the Herrán Report, has been allowed to dismiss as false the articles of Steer and, by extension, of Monks and Corman, without the slightest contribution of evidence or scientific criteria. But this is part of the Genealogy of the Lie, whose transmission requires the repetition of apocryphal news and the omission of data contradicting the "alternative truth."

Chapter 6

Gernika was bombed, but the destruction was mainly due to the action of the Italian planes

One of the characteristics of lying is its capacity for transformation and its consequent multiplicity. Once Franco ordered the lie, and a double version of the facts was spread, the skein of falsehoods became complicated to such an extent that the most extravagant variations on the same theme began to appear. Just as the coup members decided to place all the blame for the bombing on the Germans, the Germans tried to blame Gernika's destruction on the Italians.

In a report dated May 18, 1937, Colonel Erwin Jaenecke, Richthofen's assistant, asserted that "the city of Eibar, with its numerous arms and equipment factories, was set on fire very thoroughly by the Reds when it was abandoned, so that these important industries did not fall into the hands of the Whites. Great assets have been destroyed with it. On the contrary, Guernica was obviously destroyed by the Italians, and on the last day also by certain German bombs on bridges and cross-roads; and since the city, unlike the rest of Spain, used a lot of wood for the construction of its houses, these became fire fodder. The inhabitants had escaped and could not extinguish the fire. The 'sacred' tree, which constitutes the national sanctuary of the Basques, remained intact."[1]

Jaenecke had a peculiar way of lying. It was Richthofen who led the bombing of Eibar, and, as he stated in his diary, this town was bombed by the Italian Aviazione Legionaria, something that Jaenecke, as his assistant, undoubtedly had to have known. Moreover, Eibar was bombed 25 times between August 29, 1936, and April 25, 1937, and therefore the destruction, as in the case of Irun, was not due to the fire, as Franco had ordered to be proclaimed, but rather to the effect of the explosives and incendiary bombs dropped by the rebel planes, as well as to the constant attacks of the artillery during the last days of April 1937. In addition to the bombardments of the Italian trimotors, between April 24 and 25, Richthofen ordered that the fighter, ground assault, and reconnaissance plane squads of the Condor Legion constantly attack the roads between Eibar and Markina.[2] As Colonel Joachim von Richthofen wrote, the destruction of Eibar was due to the Italian bombings ordered by the German High Command: "The destruction was total. The effect of the explosions is projected upwards. The adjoining houses were not much affected. The repeated attacks from a height of only 600 to 800 meters, which was possible in virtue of the absence of any type of anti-aircraft or ground defense, also met their mark. They were favored by the Italian launch procedure and the degree of destruction reached amounted to 60 percent."[3] Apart from the material destruction, the attacks on Eibar caused a high number of fatalities; in particular, the Basque government recorded 74 dead and 97 injured in April alone.[4] As Richthofen laconically explained, the Italians bombarded Eibar "by mistake," so "it burns a little."[5]

Jaenecke, who coordinated the activity of the Condor Legion and the Aviazione Legionaria under Richthofen, knew therefore that on April 25, seven Italian trimotors had bombarded Eibar, launching a large number of explosive and incendiary bombs. Jaenecke was also perfectly aware that the Condor Legion had bombed Gernika and that the number of Italian aircraft involved in the bombing was substantially less than that of German aircraft. However, he decided to blame the destruction of Gernika on the Italians and to blame the destruction of Eibar on the "Reds." Moreover, even though, according to him, Gernika "was obviously destroyed by the Italians," he concluded in his report that "per se, Guernica was a resounding success of the German air weapon. The only retreat route from the entire Red Coast was cut in full mode by the fire and a pile of debris two meters high on the roads."[6] But, apart from the fact that if Gernika had been destroyed by the Italians, the credit for this "achievement" should have been theirs, Jaenecke never explained why the bombing was a "resounding success" when the alleged main objective of the attack, the bridge of Errenteria by which the Basque troops were supposedly retreating, suffered no damage.

Based on Jaenecke's writings, Karl Drumm constructed a new version of what took place on April 26 in Gernika, a town that, according to the author, is at the bottom of a deep fjord:

Shortly after the destructive bombing of the national sanctuary of the Basques in Gernika was carried out, the issue was magnified disproportionately as a heinous crime by the world press. The city of Guernica is at the end of a deep fjord; and here there was a bridge of strategic importance, since it was the only line of communication between the positions of the Red troops located to the south with their control zone. The destruction of the bridge was the main objective of that day's operations. The Condor Legion had sent its bombers to attack the bridge separately, and as soon as the bombs began to fall, people in town were immediately evacuated and fled to the hills. Then the following misfortune came to happen: the city of Gernika is located in a region rich in forests and therefore their houses, to a much greater extent than in the rest of Spain, are built with wood. Not only the Germans, but also the Italians had been ordered to bomb the bridge, but the Italians had a bombing method different from that of the Germans. Instead of flying alone, they flew in squadron formation and, at a signal from the squad leader, they dropped the entire bomb load simultaneously. As a result of this, a good part of the bombs fell far from their target, right in the center of the abandoned city. Since there was no one to put out fires, a large part of the city caught fire.[7]

Drum's version is fraudulent because of the total of 59 or 62 airplanes that participated in the bombing, only three or six were Italian (5 to 9 percent), which could only have thrown a small proportion of the total explosive over the town. Consequently, as Jaenecke and Drum perfectly knew, the Italian bombers could not have caused most of the damage. Both officials underlined the fact that the city was deserted, pretending in this way to reduce the potential number of casualties. This version allows them to explain the "fire" of Gernika through the local population's hypothetical "abandonment" of the urban nucleus, a version of the facts that Richthofen occasionally used in some of his writings.

Chapter 7

Gernika was bombed and shelled by Basque troops

The editors of the Herrán Report wrote that "on Thursday, [April] 29 soldiers of the nationalist army entered the town and in the following days the Red army, defeated, bombed the city and the Red aviators tried to bomb it."[1] Apart from not being properly written, this claim lacks veracity given the fact that the Republican government did not have bombers in the area. More specifically, from April 15 to May 1, the Republican air force did not act on any of the fronts of Bizkaia.

In this case, the lie originates in the testimony of Domingo Hormaeche, an informant whose testimony was included in the Herrán Report. According to this witness, the Reds had bombed Gernika with incendiary bombs produced in the village itself. Hormaeche declared

> "[t]hat by the official order of the Basque Government there were constructed in said workshops from the month of November 19, 6 fuses for incendiary bombs, and that trials were made with certain of these, from which it emerged that the body of the bomb was made in Bilbao in the Talleres Jemein, Errasti & Cerritagoitia in Castaños Street. [. . .] The incendiary bombs dropped over Guernica were dropped by the Reds. [. . .] In his opinion the incendiary bombs which caused the burning of several houses during the bombing were dropped by Red aeroplanes, a deduction which he makes from the results which these bombs produced, and that the explosions throughout the night of the 26th to the 27th must have been produced by dynamite, as the noise which they caused could be heard at a distance of five kilometres.[2]

Among other irregularities, the witness never explained how he knew that the detonations were heard five kilometers away when he himself was in Gernika.

Richthofen went further by stating literally and without shame that, days after the occupation of Gernika by the national troops, "the city was bombed four times by the Red air force and also shelled for quite some time by the Red artillery."[3] He was perfectly aware that the Basque government had no airplanes in the area, and he knew that the Republican aviation stationed on the fronts of Cantabria and Asturias had not acted on the Basque front during the last two weeks of April. In particular, Richthofen was aware that the Basque government had never owned bombing planes and that at the beginning of the campaign there were only eight Polikarpov I-15 fighter planes stationed at the Lamiako airfield in Leioa.[4] He also knew that he had ordered eighteen consecutive aerial bombardments and machine-gunning on this air base between April 6 and May 16, 1937, as a result of which all these devices were shot down or neutralized on the ground.

Chapter 8

It was a strategic bombing whose objective was the Errenteria bridge

The first version of the reductionist discourse, stating that only eight explosive bombs had been dropped on Gernika, was not credible; however, this initial acceptance of the bombing was widely disseminated during the second half of the 20th century and gave rise to several different versions of the events. The version that it was a strategic bombing whose objective was the destruction of the Errenteria bridge is still defended today.

The premise is that it was a strategic or even tactical bombing, but not a terror bombing. A tactical bombing is an air strike on targets of immediate military interest in the context of a battle, such as troops, installations, or military equipment that are actively engaged in battle. A variant of tactical bombings is an aerial interdiction bombing, or an aerial attack against targets distant of the battlefield but still part of the theater of operations. In the case of Gernika, German planes would have provided close air support to the attacking rebel forces by destroying the withdrawal routes of the Basque troops. A strategic bombing, on the other hand, is an air mission independent of naval or land operations, directed against military objectives located far from the combat zones, such as factories, communications hubs, or airports. A terror bombing is an air mission whose purpose is to destroy the morale of the enemy and, consequently, to provoke its surrender through an intense and unexpected attack against a target of great symbolic value. The effectiveness of terror bombings is proportional to the level of material destruction. Open or defenseless cities with a large influx of civilians are in general the targets of terror bombing attacks.

Several authors have stressed that the bombing of Gernika could not be a terror bombing since the Condor Legion had as its "supreme motto" respect for civilians. Richthofen, Sperrle, and the Italian command emphasized this fact, going so far as to falsify the orders, records, and dispatches, as noted by Captain Ehrhart K. Dellmensingen, commander of the third squadron of Junkers Ju 52 bombers that attacked Gernika.[1] Rolf-Dieter Müller asserted in 2008 that "the offensive carried out by some dozens of German and Italian planes over the small Basque city of Gernika, on April 26, 1937, was not planned in any way as a terror bombing. Its objective was to strangle the battlefield to prevent the retreat of the republican troops. For this, at the request of the Nationalist command, a bridge located on the outskirts of the city and the roads leading to it had to be destroyed."[2] Corum also wrote that "the Condor Legion bombed Guernica as a routine tactical air operation."[3] He seemed to refer to a strategic action or an air interdiction operation but, in any case, author insisted on emphasizing that it was a "routine" action.

The goal of asserting that it was a strategic bombing or an air interdiction operation is therefore to mask the nature of the attack. Logically, in order to turn the bombing of Gernika into a strategic bombing, it is necessary to find a strategic objective within the limits of Gernika, and this is not easy. Despite the official version that Gernika had not been bombed, Franco himself was one of the first to state that "first line units [the Spanish command] directly requested aerial bombing of crossroads, executed by German and Italian air units."[4] The difficulty in giving credibility to this version lies in the fact that, although the armament factories that were in the village, the dormitories for the out-of-service Basque soldiers or the Errenteria bridge could be considered legitimate military targets, none of these was touched during the bombing. Consequently, the authors who have defended this thesis are forced to generate a new lie in order to explain why after three and a half hours of bombing and after the release of tons of explosives and incendiary bombs, these legitimate military target objectives were not achieved. In fact, as Colonel Meise said in a report signed on March 21, 1938, that "during the withdrawal to Asturias, the pilots had to destroy the bridge of Guernica, in order to cut off the Red retreat. The bridge does not show the impact of a splinter and remains intact. Guernica, on the other hand, has been reduced to ashes and rubble, a picture more horrible than Alberich's destructions during his retreat to the Siegfried front in 1917."[5]

Salas was among the authors who supported this version and, following Richthofen, he wrote that the bombing of Gernika was intended to destroy the Errenteria bridge with the tactical objective of bagging the Basque battalions in retreat. Other authors, such as Adolf Galland, a Heinkel He 51 pilot of the Condor Legion, and Vicente Talón, argued that the objective of the bombing was to destroy the Errenteria bridge, but not necessarily apprehend retreating troops, as a legitimate strategic objective in itself.[6] Finally, Rolf-Dieter Müller referred to the destruction of "the railway bridge,"[7] although there has never been a railway bridge in Gernika. The reason for this error lies, as in many other cases, in the use of historical sources that lack credibility.

In reference to Gernika, Galland incorporated into the Spanish version of his book the ideas of Richthofen, Sperrle, Ribbentrop, and Göring:

> In the first months of the intervention, the Condor bombers had been ordered to destroy a road bridge by which the Reds transported their troops and large quantities of war material to the tenaciously defended industrial city and port of Bilbao. The attack was verified under poor visibility conditions, with primitive pointing devices. As the columns of smoke from the bombs dropped by the squadrons dissipated, the bridge remained unscathed, but a village beside it had suffered considerable damage. Enemy war materiel had also been destroyed, but overall the action could be considered a failure, all the more so as the objective of our operations was to achieve the destruction of the enemy, with special respect for the civilian population.[8]

Consequently, according to Galland, the error was therefore due to two factors. On the one hand, the smoke produced by the explosions of the first bombing squadrons made visibility impossible, so the Ju 52 Junkers who attacked in second and third place dropped their bombs blindly, without intention to destroy the urban area. On the other hand, airplanes at that time did not have adequate instruments to carry out such a precise attack. Jesús Salas and Ferdinando Pedriali pointed out that, due to the technical limitations of the airplanes of that era, it is not surprising that the bombers missed their targets.[9]

Pete T. Cenarrusa, instructor of naval aviators in dive-bombing techniques between 1942 and 1945, studied the location, structure, and dimensions of the Errenteria bridge and estimated that a static target of those dimensions and characteristics could have been destroyed by dive bombing and dropping a single 250-kilogram bomb:

> As a Curtiss pilot and dive bombing instructor, I attest that the destruction of a static military target of the dimensions of the Errenteria bridge requires a single ground-attack aircraft, designed to perform dive bombings such as the Junkers Ju 87 or the Henschel Hs 123, models available to the Condor Legion in the spring of 1936 – which were not chosen to be used in Gernika. The number and type of aircraft involved in the bombing of Gernika, the flight formation adopted by them, as well as the mixture of explosive bombs launched on the city center and the fact that incendiary bombs were used and the civilian population was machine-gunned – added to the expense involved in the mobilization of said air force – make it possible to ensure that the objective was not the aforementioned bridge of Errenteria and that, consequently, it was not a strategic bombing but a terror bombing whose purpose was the total destruction of the city.[10]

F. Willard Robinson, pilot of a TBM-3E Avenger and author of *Navy Wings of Gold*, fully agreed with Cenarrusa and said that "it is totally illogical" to assume that it was a strategic bombing intended to destroy a bridge of the dimensions of the one in Errenteria.[11]

War veteran Phil Reberger also said that if one of his pilots had returned from a bombing mission without even having touched the bridge after having launched a minimum of 31 tons of bombs, he would not have flown in the rest of the war. Although Müller stated bluntly that "the number of bombers, as well as the quantity of incendiary bombs used, remained within the usual limits in the attacks on bridges,"[12] Robinson, Reberger, and Chuck Winder agree in affirming that:

1. The standard procedure for blowing a bridge (about 70 feet long and 32 feet wide) from the air, in an open town with no anti-aircraft batteries or any other defenses (such as pursuit planes), does not involve 24 bombers and 23 fighters launching a total of between thirty and forty tons of bombs (at least a third of them incendiary) for three and a half hours.[13]
2. That destroying a bridge of such characteristics is a simple static target that could be achieved with a single dive bomber or even with a bomber.

3. That, in view of the results (the bridge was not even touched, and the city was completely destroyed with a result of 74 percent of all buildings demolished),[14] it seems that the real aim of the bombing was not to destroy the bridge but to drive the Basques to surrender.[15]

In April 1937 the Condor Legion had Junkers Ju 87 (*Stuka*)[16] and Henschels Hs 123 dive-bomber planes but, as indicated by Cenarrusa, the four Henschel Hs 123 stationed at the air base of Gasteiz, less than 15 minutes of flight from Gernika, were precisely the only ones that Richthofen left on the ground in the course of the bombing. Cenarrusa concluded that the Errenteria bridge was not destroyed because the air command "did not want the bridge to be touched or damaged, in any way."[17] In fact, according to Salas, out of a total of 32 impacts of 250-kilogram bombs registered in Gernika, 27 were more than 250 meters away from said bridge.[18] In response to Galland, Salas, and Pedriali's excuses based on the supposed technical limitations of the devices of the time, Cenarrusa said that "to point out that after throwing between 31 and 46 tons of bombs, the bridge could not be reached is as much as affirming that they were completely incompetent pilots, too inept to be minimally credible."[19] In fact, contrary to the opinion of Salas and Pedriali, the Henschel Hs 123 dive bombers could attack not only static targets but also objects in motion and smaller than a bridge. For example, on May 22, 1940, a unit of Henschel Hs 123 attacked in the vicinity of Cambrai, with great success, a unit of 40 French tanks in motion, achieving direct impacts on several of them and forcing the withdrawal of the unit.

It is obvious that the characteristics of the bombing are not those of an air attack against a bridge. The destruction of a bridge from the air does not require the participation of a minimum of 32 fighters and 27 bombers, nor the release of 32 to 46 tons of explosive, nor does it imply the use of incendiary bombs, nor the aerial strafing of the civilian population for three and a half hours. This version is so absurd that even Major Robert Fuchs, commander of the bombing group K/88 of Burgos, and Ehrhart K. Dellmensingen, commander of the third squadron of Junkers Ju 52 bombers that attacked Gernika, had to admit that carrying boxes with incendiary bombs arranged in the interior corridor of planes to be thrown by hand was not typical of an operation that had supposedly aimed at a bridge. In the words of Dellmensingen himself, "When I was denied permission to modify the load [and remove these boxes of incendiary bombs] I said: Well, let's suppose they are wooden bridges."[20]

Finally, Salas again fell short of the truth by saying that delay fuses are suitable for destroying bridges: "To this must be added the problem of fuses. There were two types: contact fuses and delayed fuses. The contact fuse makes the bomb explode at the same time as it hits the ground. They are good for destroying everything that is part of the superstructure. However, they are not worth destroying bridges."[21] But the use of bombs with delay fuses is neither necessary nor appropriate to destroy bridges, since the objective is the surface itself (the superstructure), which in this case is flat and smooth, so it is not necessary to penetrate inside to destroy it – much less in the case of a bridge like the one in Errenteria, which was based on only two pillars.

In view of everything mentioned above, Castor Uriarte, municipal architect of Gernika, concluded that

my biggest surprise was knowing what had not been destroyed in Gernika. There were several legitimate military objectives: the bridge between Errenteria and Gernika, the battalions of Basque soldiers in the college of the Augustinians and in the convent of La Merced, the railway line between Gernika and Bilbao and, of course, the weapons factories. Among them the Unceta factory, which manufactured pistols, and the two buildings of Talleres de Guernica, which manufactured aviation bombs and other ammunition. As far as I know, no bomb fell near any of the soldiers' barracks or in the armament and ammunition factories, even though they were ideally located to serve as targets for the bombers. The Errenteria bridge was not damaged, although it was close to the city center and the bombs fell around it. And the railroad between Gernika and Bilbao? Sometime after midnight, evacuees boarded special trains south of the Gernika train station, and moved to Bilbao. The truth is that I do not know anything of a significant military nature that was destroyed in the bombing."[22]

Chapter 9

It was a strategic bombing whose objective was to cut the withdrawal to the Basque troops

Some authors have emphasized that Gernika was a "legitimate" military objective because it was a "very important" crossroad and communications hub. In this sense, the telegram from the General Headquarters of Salamanca to Hugo Sperrle of May 7, 1937, stated that "Guernica, a village of less than five thousand souls, was six kilometers away from the line of combat; it is a very important communications junction, it has a factory, ammunition, bombs and guns; [on] the 26th it was the place [of] passage [for the] units in retreat and [the place for the] station of the reserves."[1]

Richthofen himself was one of the first people to propose this explanation for the bombing of Gernika, noting in his diary that he tried to capture the Basque forces in the area between Gerrikaitz and Gernika by destroying the bridge of Errenteria and town's road network.[2] By destroying the bridge "through which the Reds transported their troops and large quantities of war material," these battalions in retreat would be surrounded and, without means of retreat, trapped: "[Colonel Juan] Vigón pledges his word that he will print to his troops a pace such that all roads south of Guernica will be blocked. If we get it, we have the enemy in the bag around Marquina."[3]

In a report on the experiences of the Condor Legion, Richthofen repeated this idea in more detail:

The Red front, located for long months southeast of Bilbao, had now been broken in an area of 25 kilometers. The remaining positions, particularly the left wing, by the sea, continued impassively, which clearly enabled the separation of larger enemy groups by means of a rapid advance to the northwest on Guernica. At the breaking front, the enemy retreated to the west and northwest. The brigades were now driven northwest by all means possible; the air units had to delay the enemy's retreat by means of constant attacks on the crossroads and the bridges, so that remaining adversary troops could be surrounded by the attacking forces. The Reds' movements were widely disrupted by concentrated air attacks, among which Guernica represented the most important success.[4]

The problem with this version is that it is necessary to affirm, document, and explain that the troops retreated towards Bilbao through Gernika, so the authors who have defended this version have emphasized that Gernika was "an important crossroads" or "an important communication node." Also, it is necessary to document that there was a plan for the "bagging" of the retreating Basque troops.

But neither the one nor the other is true.

In the first place, there is no documentary evidence of a supposed operation to capture Basque troops in retreat in any of the official war parties' plans at the end of April, and there is no evidence that Colonel Vigón promised Richthofen to issue such an order. Neither the general plan of operations in Bizkaia at the end of March 1937, nor the general order to initiate the invasion of Bizkaia on March 29, nor the order for the collaboration and support of the air forces with the brigades of Navarre on March 31, nor the operations parts of the Navarre brigades, nor the orders or summaries of the April 25 or 26 operations of any of the three ground forces involved in the conflict made any mention of this alleged plan. Quite the opposite, the order of operations of the Navarre brigades for April 25 clearly states that the objective of these units was not to advance toward Gernika but to take "the enemy positions between Eibar and Marquina,"[5] that is, to advance in the direction opposite to that of Richthofen's alleged plan.

In fact, contrary to what Richthofen asserted, it was not the Navarrese brigades advancing towards Gernika but the Italian units that operated in the coastal sector, so the aforementioned "bagging" should figure in the orders or plans of these units of infantry. But in the report on the operations of the northern front in the last days of April that General Bastico sent to Count Galeazzo Ciano, he does not mention this plan. Rather, on the contrary, Bastico reported that his units would advance through Berriz on Mount Oiz and take Etxebarria, and that from there, they would advance towards Durango and occupy this town and Markina, establishing the front on the line dividing Iurreta, Aulesti, and Lekeitio. Later, they would continue the advance on the front in Orozko (from the south), Amorebieta (from the east), and Gernika (from the northeast and southeast).[6] In summary, the report of the Italian units clearly states that the advance on Gernika would be carried out from Ereño (to the northeast) and through Gerrikaitz and Aulesti (to the southeast), that is, from the front lines in Lekeitio and in Markina.

Along these same lines, General Vincenzo Velardi, head of the Aviazione Legionaria, wrote in a report to the secretary of state signed on May 6, 1937, that the advance of the Italian infantry was ready for April 28, and not for day 26, as Richthofen suggested, and stressed that this maneuver was organized "in full and direct agreement with the German and Spanish air force command,"[7] that is, with Richthofen and Kindelán.

And the advance of the Francoist units was obviously conducted in accordance with the reports referred to. The Italian units advanced towards Gernika from Lekeitio and Markina, and the Navarrese brigades advanced towards Durango and Zornotza through Eibar. No enclosing movement was ever attempted.

Indeed, the involvement maneuver Richthofen referred to in his diary was totally impracticable. Capturing the light infantry battalions defending the northeastern and eastern sectors of the Basque front would have required the Navarre brigades to advance at a speed between twenty and thirty times higher than that registered up to that date. From the beginning of the spring offensive on March 31, 1937, until April 28, the Francoist forces had advanced northward at an average of just one kilometer a day and about half a kilometer daily to the east. Richthofen was perfectly aware of this fact and repeatedly criticized Mola for the slowness of the rebel advance. And, more specifically, on April 26, the rebel troops were exhausted, and their right flank totally uncovered, given that the fourth brigade had not advanced the previous day, nor was it even able to take the 816 summit of Mount Oiz, which was the objective marked for that day.[8]

Richthofen's alleged maneuver would have required that the brigades south of Mount Oiz advance towards the summit and, surrounding it, take Gernika before the Basque battalions pushed by the Italian units in the area of Lekeitio arrived at the village. In parallel, it would have also required that the Navarrese brigades take Durango in order to stop the retreat of the Basque battalions towards Bilbao. All this involved covering the mountain through the approximately 32 kilometers that separates Berriz and Gernika – through Albiz and Elejalde – in a single day.[9]

Apart from all this, it is materially impossible to stop twelve battalions of light infantry by blowing up a bridge of the dimensions of Errenteria, on a river that barely reaches one and a half meters deep. Infantry units could have forded the Oka River at many points. Moreover, the Basque troops could have been transported through the railway line that crosses Gernika and joins it with Zornotza. However, this communication route between Gernika and Bilbao to the south was never attacked, and Richthofen never made any reference to its strategic value.

In view of all this, some authors have suggested that, in order to cut off the withdrawal of the Basque troops, Richthofen sought to obstruct the retreat of the twelve Basque battalions by destroying the road network of the interior of Gernika. This is equally absurd since there are at least five roads that flank Gernika in any direction without any need to cross the city center. Proof of all this is that Richthofen himself pointed out in his diary that the day after the bombing "(rather intense) traffic is heading, on the east side of Guernica, to the southwest."[10]

Lies sometimes take unexpected turns. Reporter Pierre Hericourt noted that the access roads to Gernika, the bridge and the train tracks had not been touched and concluded that this fact constituted irrefutable proof that Gernika had been set on fire by the "Reds," since after a bombing intended to apprehend retreating troops, the roads would logically have been attacked and affected.[11]

But, apart from all the above, the hypothesis that the troops would be captured in their withdrawal through Gernika is completely illogical because of the simple fact that the twelve Basque battalions defending the front should not be withdrawn through Gernika to the north but to the south, towards Zornotza. And in fact, they did so, simply because they did not have to pass through Gernika on their way to Bilbao. In addition to the fact that the road through Durango and Zornotza is the shortest route to Bilbao, by retreating from the sector of Markina to Bilbao through Gerrikaitz and Zornotza the Basque units maintained the front line and defended their flanks from the attacking troops. Strategically, retreating through Gernika would have been disastrous, which is precisely why Sabin Apraiz, a member of the Basque army's

Joint Chiefs of Staff, ordered the battalions to retreat through Zornotza and, fundamentally, not to retreat through Gernika, which indicates, beyond all reasonable doubt, that it was neither necessary nor convenient to cross Gernika to reach the positions of the Iron Belt around Bilbao.[12]

Based on this, we can infer that Richthofen lied when mentioning an operation for capturing troops that was never planned nor intended to be carried out because it would have been materially impossible.

Colonel Jaenecke wrote that Guernica had been a resounding success because the only retreat route for the Basque troops had been cut in full by the fire and a pile of debris two meters high on the roads.[13] Colonel Wilhelm Meise repeated this in 1938.[14] And Corum, quoting Richthofen, expressed the same idea:

> On 30 April, von Richthofen visited Guernica just after it fell to the Nationalist forces. In his diary he made a few laconic remarks, and none of them referred to any success in terrorizing the Basques. He noted that in most respects the attack had been a success. The town had been 'leveled' and 'the city was completely closed to traffic for twenty-four hours.' This was, indeed, the effect he was trying to achieve. Von Richthofen also noted that the attack had been a real technical success in terms of the effectiveness of the Luftwaffe's new 250-kilogram bombs and the EC B I bomb fuse.[15]

But this is not true either. Traffic over the Errenteria bridge and through the village itself remained continuous and very active. Both Jaenecke and Richthofen knew perfectly well that the "bagging" never materialized nor had the "only route of withdrawal" been obstructed. Richthofen himself explained this, arguing that "nevertheless, given that the national brigades pursued the Red enemy slowly, they managed at the last moment, moving very close to their own front, to safely install to the west of Guernica the whole of their material and the most of their soldiers."[16]

Apart from all this, Richthofen never explained that Colonel Juan Vigón, who according to his own testimony "had pledged his word" (which is neither documented nor plausible without the consent of General Emilio Mola and Franco), but did not fulfill it.

And the lie has been perpetuated.

Lieutenant Hans von Beust, commander of the second K/88 squad of Junkers Ju 52 that bombed Gernika, stated in 1955, and later corroborated with a supplementary writing of March 16, 1973, that "at that time the Reds flowed all along from the coast to the west, in retreat towards the Iron Belt [Bilbao], with the intention of creating new lines of defense there. This retreat led a good number of them through Guernica, which was overflowing with enemy troops, and over a small bridge very close to it, to the south. This bridge, and the troops that piled on it, were the objective set by the command; the reconnaissance units had been informed of that situation [. . .]. As can be seen in my report, the targets were these movements of troops, not in the city, but the access roads."[17]

To this day, Salas, Talón, and Corum, among others, have repeated this version without any other documentary contribution than Richthofen's and Jaenecke's references. Corum has explained that "[i]n April 1937 [Gernika] was located just behind the front lines of the Basque army. Its importance at the time was clear on the map. The Basque army was being pressed hard by the Nationalist forces, and Guemica had a bridge and an important road intersection that was vital for the withdrawal of twenty three battalions of Basque army troops located east of Guernica. If the route through Guernica could be closed, the Basque forces would be hindered in their retreat to the heavily forti-fied defenses around Bilbao and could be cut off and destroyed."[18]

Talón simply repeated Richthofen's version, affirming without any documentary support that "the natural movement of the defenders of Vizcaya, in that sector, was to fall back on the provincial town, as many did, while there were those who opposed this initiative, perhaps because they believed, with very good sense, that Guernica could become, under the wings of airplanes, a deadly trap."[19] On the contrary, Salas, under-standing that this plan was completely impracticable, wrote that Richthofen was dominated by "an overflowing optimism" when he suggested the idea of capturing the Basque units in retreat.[20] In fact, Salas, knowing that the alleged "bagging" required an impossible speed of advance, stated in his book that the first brigade was to achieve "a slight additional progression towards Guernica,"[21] but did not mention that the said advance rate, of between twenty and thirty times greater than the one registered up until that day, is more than "light."[22] And immediately afterwards, he added that the incapability of apprehending the Basque troops generated "a new fight" between Generals Mola and Richthofen, of which obviously there is no documentary evidence. Salas was aware that there was no order in relation to the alleged capture, so he concludes that "this dispute would lead to the drama of Guernica and its complete practical uselessness,"[23] suggesting that, despite the fact that General Mola never planned nor ordered a bagging maneuver, Richthofen acted on his own and undertook the bombing, which explains that nothing happened as he planned.

Even though the withdrawal was not interrupted, and the Basque units neither withdrew through Gernika nor were bagged, and none of the alleged military objectives such as the bridge were destroyed, nor were the roads obstructed, nor the crossroads destroyed, the falsehood that Gernika was an "important hub" is still being repeated.

Chapter 10

Gernika was a legitimate military objective because . . .

Many authors have claimed that Gernika was a legitimate military objective, insisting on the fact that it was not an open city. An open city is a location without an armed defense system or fortification structures. The absence of a defense system means that this population will not be defended with weapons and, therefore, it is assumed that the advancing army will occupy it without bloodshed and will not attack it by land or from the air.

Some German and Spanish officers, and later several authors, have alluded to the knot of roads, the railroad track, the presence of soldiers, the existence of barracks and weapons factories, and even the ammunition stores. But the truth is that what turns a locality into an open city is not the presence or absence of troops or other military objectives in its interior, but rather the existence of troops willing to defend it or the existence of fortification systems of defense, all of which Gernika was completely lacking.

Both Franco and Richthofen declared that Gernika was a legitimate military objective because "some roads for the retreat of the Reds north of Marquina converge east of Guernica."[1] Franco himself, in a telegram sent to General Sperrle on May 7, 1937, stated that the frontline units of the Spanish command directly had requested that the German and Italian air forces bomb the "crossroads" of Gernika.[2] Hans von Beust, head of the second Junkers squadron that bombarded Gernika, said that "the city itself was a perfect military objective – if so understood – for the accumulation of troops in it."[3]

A telegram from the General Headquarters of Salamanca to the commander of the Condor Legion, General Sperrle, dated May 7, 1937, referred to the geostrategic importance of Gernika, assuring that it was six kilometers from the front, when the situation report No. 252 on

April 28 drafted by the Information Service of the Navy of the German High Command had detailed that the village was 18 kilometers from the front. The document also underlined the "very important" strategic relevance of Gernika and the existence of weapons factories.[4] Corrado Ricci, Fiat Cr.32 pilot who participated in the bombing, stated for instance that "Guernica is an important elevation: in its neighborhoods the Reds have entrenched themselves solidly, in the city there is a large contingent of soldiers and the troops fight well."[5] All this is false. There were no solid trenches in Gernika, nor was there ever a great contingent in the village, and Gernika has never been an elevation, since it is located 10 meters above sea level.

This version of the lie has been repeated. Talón wrote that on April 26, 1937, the plaza was of the greatest strategic interest and thus became a military objective. According to the author, "through Guernica there was a narrow-gauge railway directly linked to the front line and six important roads leading to town, which was, at the same time, a place for the cantonment of military reserves."[6] Salas similarly stated that "no one will doubt that Guernica was the key point of the Basque front from April 25 to mid-May and a tactical objective of most importance."[7] More recently, Corum has written that "[a]t least two Basque army battalions were stationed in Guernica, the 18th Loyala Battalion and the Saseta Battalion. The Nationalists were also rightly concerned that the Basques might turn Guernica into a fortified position. By all the rules of international warfare in 1937, Guemica was a legitimate target for aerial attack [. . .]. Well before the German attack, Guernica had been singled out for special attention by von Richthofen because of its importance in the Basque road network."[8] But the author does not give any documentary evidence of Richthofen's references to Gernika prior to April 25, 1937.

By virtue of the most elementary legal principles of war, the mere presence of factories does not turn a city or a town into a legitimate target, as Franco, Richthofen, von Beust, or Ricci suggested and as Salas, Talón, or Corum have written more recently. By pure logic, the legitimate targets are the weapons factories, the road junctions, and the barracks themselves, not the civilian population. But not one of the aforementioned authors explains that none of these alleged "legitimate objectives," existing (weapons factory) or nonexistent (railway bridge), real (Errenteria bridge) or unreal (weapons deposits or barracks), was damaged. Moreover, none of the above-mentioned authors ever states that the bombing of the bridge and the communication hubs, the railroad, the barracks,[9] and the arms factories were avoided and so never damaged. Moreover, the Condor Legion and the Legionary Aviazione were violating with their mere presence the Non-intervention Pact, ratified by Germany and Italy in August 1937. So, from a strictly legal perspective, the bombing of Gernika, like any of the other bombings perpetrated by the rebel units, was, per se, illegitimate and illegal.

In sum, as General Bastico declared, the Second Mixed Brigade and the Fourth Brigade entered Gernika at noon on April 29 without firing a shot, because Gernika, like any other open city, was not defended.[10]

From a very particular standpoint, Machimbarrena and Miláns del Bosch asserted that Gernika was not a military objective but that, if the Francoist forces had wanted to bomb Gernika, they would have done so because, from their perspective, that is what happens in war:

> It has been said, with good reason, that Guernica was not a military objective of such importance to make this display of destruction to be acceptable. One might think that they wanted to punish Basque separatism in the city where the traditional tree stands, but apart from the fact that this claim is unfounded and that this kind of revenge goes against the ethic of Generalissimo Franco's armies, it turns out that the among the little things still standing are the famous tree and the buildings surrounding it.[11]

General Queipo de Llano also stated that Gernika was not a military objective, but he assured Radio Sevilla that it was legitimate to bomb it as any other target in the course of the war. However, in Queipo de Llano's view, hospitals were also legitimate military targets. In fact, on Saturday, October 24, 1936, he threatened to bomb hospitals,[12] and a few days later there were a number of air strikes on several of them, such as the one that took place on October 25 against the military hospital in Markina.[13]

Müller affirmed that "according to the current conception" "the German bombing constituted a legitimate military operation. Even the future Marshal of the Air Arthur Harris recognized in his memoirs that during the Second World War [that] the allies similarly bombarded urban cross-streets in order to prevent the advance or withdrawal of the Wehrmacht."[14] Machimbarrena and Miláns del Bosch had asserted the same thing a few years before: "It is foolish to scream blue murder because the air force bombed cities ... in order to prevent the army from quickly achieving such an overarching and decisive objective in this war as the occupation of Bilbao."[15] This strange way of thinking suggests that it is legitimate to bomb to the ground a city center in which a weekly market is being held and machine-gun the survivors or destroy hospitals, resulting in civilian casualties, if doing so will obstruct the withdrawal of enemy troops.

We can only hope that within the United Nations committee responsible for drafting the laws of war there are not many people who think like Machimbarrena and Miláns del Bosch . . . or Richthofen.

Al portador de este carnet

Sr. D. Godofredo
Schulze-Blanck

se autoriza libre circulación por todo el territorio ocupado por el Ejército Nacional. Se ruega a todas las autoridades civiles y militares le presten toda clase de facilidades, manifestándose al mismo tiempo que dicho señor está autorizado a llevar armas.

De orden de S. E.
El Tte. Coronel de

Escuadrilla de caza

Firma del interesado:

Unidad: Teniente

Photo 1   As U.S. ambassador Claude Bowers noted in 1936, the Non-intervention Committee, far from avoiding Italian and German intervention, regulated it in order to avoid the outbreak of an open international war. Both the Republican government and the Basque government published photographs of German and Italian POWs in order to "document" the participation of these regimes in favor of Franco. In the photo, the German fighter pilot's license of Godofredo Schulze-Blank is irrefutable proof of the active foreign participation in the conflict.

Photo 2 General Emilio Mola swore on his honor in January 1937 that there was not a single German infantry company in the rebel Army. The photo depicts a poster praising the alliance between Nazi Germany and Franco's Spain during the celebrations of victory at the end of the war.

Photo 3 Hugo Sperrle, first leader of the Condor Legion, the Luftwaffe unit sent to the war in support of the Francoist troops. In 1937, 89 percent of Franco's air force was of German or Italian origin.

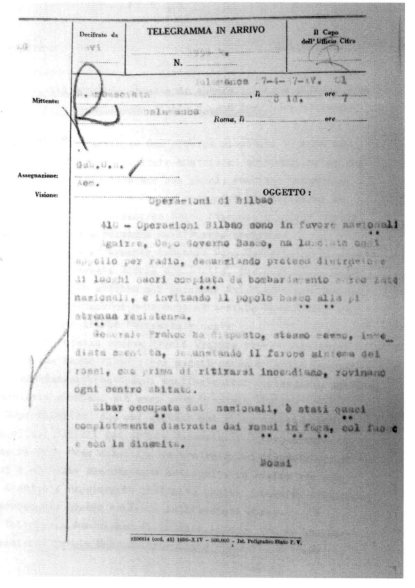

Photo 4 Telegram from diplomat Carlo Bossi to the Ministry of Foreign Affairs in Rome transmitting Franco's order to deny that aerial bombings took place and ordering him in turn to denounce the systematic destruction by fire "of all the urban centers" by the Reds in their retreat.

Photo 5 Iconic photograph of the Francoist lie that shows drums of gasoline in front of the church of San Juan, supposedly used to set Gernika afire. These containers belonged to the gas station situated next to the church.

Photo 6   The Errenteria bridge, 20 feet wide and 40 feet long. Allegedly, 59 planes were used – half of them fighters – and 31 to 46 tons of bombs were dropped for three and a half hours to destroy that bridge. However, it remained intact.

Photo 7   Ruins of Gernika. As shown in the report by the architect Gonzalo Cárdenas, 85.22 percent of the buildings in Gernika, a total of 271, were totally destroyed. The rest suffered serious damage affecting between 25 and 75 percent of the structures. Only one percent of the buildings were spared – the weapons factories and the houses of notorious pro-Francoists.

Photo 8   As a result of the incendiary bombs, the wooden interior of the houses collapsed completely while some of the exterior walls of the buildings, much thicker and built in stone, remained standing.

Photo 9 Some people were buried alive under tons of rubble. People who were in underground shelters and survived the explosions resulting from the bombing, became trapped in them and died of suffocation, or were devoured by the fires that spread through the urban center.

Photo 10 "I ran into a good woman... who could not say anything but 'My son, my son'. She dragged me to the pile of rubble that had been her house. I started working like a madman, removing stones and heavy wooden beams. I scratched my nails until I broke them... When I touched the clothes of that creature that was not more than three years old, I stained my hands with his still hot blood. I took that broken and lifeless body and raised him to his mother." Testimony of the gudari Joseba Elosegi.

Photo 11 "I joined those who were working, but it was useless. We could hear people under the rubble, calling and moaning, and we were working as hard as we could. But there was too much debris on them and the fires were increasing in size and getting closer and closer. Finally, we had to abandon them. At that moment, I almost went crazy." Testimony of Sabin Apraiz.

Photo 12   This photograph shows that the bombing was surgically accurate. The train track at the bottom of the photograph, scarcely 20 meters wide, separates the part totally destroyed by the bombs (such as the railway station) from the part that was not affected at all (such as the weapons factories). The streets of San Juan and Portu, which were barely six meters wide, in the right part of the photograph, separate with great precision the parts totally destroyed (to the left) from those that were not affected (to the right or north of these streets). Also, the streets of Asilo Calzada and Allende Salazar separate the destroyed areas from those not destroyed (in the upper part of the photograph, east of the town).

Photo 13   Some commentators have pointed out that it was impossible to destroy a bridge from the air since the bombing accuracy at the time was imprecise. Despite this, the Portugalete bridge was bombarded and damaged from the air, as shown in this photograph taken by Italian reconnaissance aircraft – an example of precision bombing.

Photo 14   Italian bombs decorated with names of Republican leaders. Between 31 and 46 tons of bombs were dropped in the city center of Gernika, an area of less than one square kilometer where between 10,000 and 12,000 civilians had gathered for the weekly market.

OBSERVATORIO DE IGUELDO

DIPUTACION DE GUIPUZCOA

Lunes 26 de abril *de 19 37* Hora *16*

| TEMPERATURA | Máxima | Mínima | Id. junto al suelo | Insolación |

Barómetro ...... *748.7* mm. ...... mb.   Viento: Dirección... *N*   Fuerza...... *3*

instrumental ......   Veleta: Dirección...   Velocidad..

744,0

−1,6

7427

nivel del mar ... *766,5*   *1012,0*

Barógrafo ......   Corrección

766,7   Id.

00
Variación en 3 h

Nubes: Cantidad total *6/10*

Clase	Cantidad	Dirección	Velocidad	Altura
Cu	*4*			*9 ur*
Al-Cu	*2*			*3 ur*

Termómetro A. *11,9*   Higrógrafo A.. *88*

Id. B. *12,6*   Id. B...

Humedad ...... *80 %*

Termómetro seco *11,6*   Tensión del vapor. *8,15*

Id. húmedo *9,9*   Evaporímetro... *9,7*

Diferencia ...... *1,7*   Lectura anterior ... *1*

Diferencia ......

Pluviómetro......
Pluviógrafo Fuess......
Id. Richard......
En 24 horas......
Comienzo de la lluvia y carácter......

	Visibilidad		
N	E	S	W
8	*8*	*8*	*8*

Meteoros

∞

Mar: Superficie *Marejadilla*
Mar de fondo *Rizada*
Dirección *NW*
Número de la clave: *3*

Telegrama *35026*   *0285 7*   *32 971 1*   *22012*   *80300*
350C_L C_M   wwVhN_L   DDFWN   BBBTT   UC_m abb   RRSV_s E   MMmm.
Zona Vizcaya: CCO − V9 − DD IV − F4.

Photo 15   Meteorological report of the Igeldo Observatory showing that on April 26 there was dense cloud at 800 and 3,000 meters, so it would have been impossible to bomb at 3,600 meters as shown in the Italian report since there would have been no visibility. Colonel Richthofen also reported that the aircraft bombed at a low altitude, from 800 meters, below the clouds.

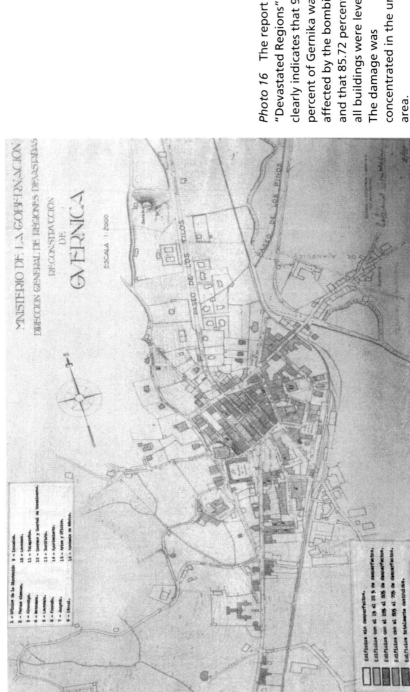

Photo 16 The report "Devastated Regions" clearly indicates that 99 percent of Gernika was affected by the bombing and that 85.72 percent of all buildings were levelled. The damage was concentrated in the urban area.

Photo 17 Remains of the shelter of Andra Mari. Between 450 and 500 people took refuge in this shelter. It received the direct impact of two 250 kilo bombs (the damage of which can be seen in the photo) as a result of which the roof and the walls of the adjacent buildings collapsed on the people who were hiding there. As Jose Labauria and Joxe Iturria testified, most of the people who sought refuge in the shelter died. Only three survivors were registered.

Photo 18 The smoking ruins. Joseba Elosegi was the first person I interviewed to write about Gernika. He told me that this photograph was taken on the morning after the bombing. He could still hear the victims' cries for help under the rubble, but nothing could be done to help them. Elosegi told me that his hands were sticky with the blood of the victims he rescued during the night. He said that the image of his hands covered in blood would remain with him all his life.

I *saw* the German 'planes bomb Guernica

— by —

NOEL MONKS

Daily Express Staff Reporter

I AM just back on leave from Bilbao—and Guernica.

Six people already have asked me: "Who DID bomb Guernica?"

I will swear to it that Franco's German aviators bombed Guernica, and that they killed 1,000 civilians.

WHEN Franco hastened to deny that his German 'planes had wrecked the ancient Basque capital, he was trying to make liars of the three accredited war correspondents who were on the spot. Another London newspaper correspondent, Reuter's correspondent, and myself.

He tried to tell us that we DIDN'T see thirty German Junker bombers flying towards Guernica at four o'clock on the afternoon of April 26 just ten minutes before, according to the stories the survivors told us later, they swooped on the defenceless town. Franco told the world there were none of "his" 'planes up that day, because of bad weather.

I'm telling the world now that there were. I saw them. My two colleagues saw them. Six thousand inhabitants of Guernica saw them. And Monday, April 26, was the sunniest day of all I spent on the Basque front.

I'm not calling Franco a liar. Maybe he didn't know the Germans were up. Franco's German allies of the air work independently of Salamanca. I think their strafe of Guernica was done entirely off their own bat.

I WAS among the ruins of Guernica one hour after the raiders had done their work, as far as I was able; the whole town was in flames.

I saw bodies in the fields spotted with machine-gun bullets, I interviewed twenty or thirty survivors. They all told the same tale. Those who could speak. Some of them could only point skywards, put their hands over their ears and rock to and fro in terror.

I went back to Bilbao and wrote my story.

I was back at Guernica at day-break. I saw 600 bodies. Nurses, children, farmers, old women, girls, old men, babies. All dead, torn and mutilated. Basque soldiers were getting the bodies from the wreckage, many of them weeping.

I came to what had been an air-raid shelter. In it were the re-mains of fifty women and children. A bomb had dropped right through the house into the cellar.

Does Franco expect the world to believe that fifty women and children fled into an air-raid shelter when their house was mined? Or trapped themselves below there while the house above them was set alight?

I WENT back to Bilbao and wrote another story, just what I had seen. Just as I would have written it if it had been a Franco town in ruins.

Then, next day came the cable from my office, reproduced above. I read it three times before I was convinced that it was serious. My two colleagues who had been with me at Guernica received similar messages. We took them in to Foreign Minister Montiguren. I'll never forget the look on his handsome face.

He shrugged his shoulders. "Gentlemen—what can I do for you? You saw really more than I or any member of my Government. Go back to Guernica, talk to whom you like. There will be no censorship today."

We all three went back to Guernica. We searched the ruined town and surrounding country-side. One of my colleagues found three dud incendiary bombs. They were German bombs, branded with the German eagle. We were more convinced than ever that the Germans had destroyed Guernica—if we needed anything more convincing than what we saw with our own eyes at four o'clock on the afternoon of April 26.

I called the office the details required, that the German

bombers we had seen near Guernica were of the heavy Junker 52 type with chasers of the Heinkel 51 type. That has never been denied.

IF Franco wanted to produce proof that the Basques destroyed their own ancient capital and murdered their own women and children, Franco has had what is left of Guernica for ten days now. I'm waiting for the "personally conducted tour" of Guernica by correspondents with Franco's forces. How well do we know these tours! I was with Franco's forces when he took Malaga. I waited for three days outside the city, with other journalists, while the Press officers went in and did a little "arranging."

Not one journalist was allowed inside Malaga until three days after it was captured. The only journalist who stayed in there until Franco came in was arrested. He is still in jail at Seville.

We correspondents at Bilbao were in Guernica before representatives of the Government were there. We saw, alone. The journalist who moves a single kilometre alone in Franco's territory is jailed at once or expelled.

AND now I'll give you a personal reason why you should not take much notice of what Franco's mouthpiece, bull-throated General Quelpo de Llano, says. Speaking from Seville the other night, on a further denial of the Guernica outrage, the general said:—

"That Señor Noel Monks. He's a drunkard. He was drunk all the time he was with our forces."

Fact is, I'm a teetotaler. Have been all my life. Ask any one who knows me. That don't ask me who bombed Guernica, I might take to drink.

Noel Monks

Photo 20   From left to right, Eusebio Arronategi, parish priest of Gernika;
Bonifacio Etxegarai, president of the Basque Court of Justice; Jose
Labauria, mayor of Gernika; and the London *Times* journalist George L.
Steer. They all testified that German planes had bombed Gernika.

Photo 21   Heroes of the Condor Legion. Detail of the Berlin victory parade published in the magazine *Der Adler* in 1939.

Photo 22 Hans J. Wandel, pilot of a Heinkel He51 ground-attack aircraft, was shot down on May 13 when he was conducting an aerial experiment: how many people he could mow down with his two machine-guns at 900, 600, and 500 meters of altitude. After his arrest he testified that he had flown over Gernika on April 26 and that the pilots had received the order "to machine-gun from the air anything that moved." After the bombing he wrote a postcard to his girlfriend Else: "Spain is a great country. We can destroy it in a few weeks. Yesterday we buried a town."

Photo 23 Wolfram von Richthofen, planner and executor of the bombing of Gernika.

Chapter 11

It was not a terror bombing

In the absence of arguments to support the hypothesis that it was a strategic bombing, some authors have denied that it was a terror bombing, without necessarily explaining why it was not.

Müller stated that "the offensive carried out by a few dozen German and Italian planes over the small Basque city of Gernika on April 26, 1937, was not planned in any way as a terror bombing."[1] And, along the same lines, Corum wrote that "despite the myths that arose around the bombing of Guernica, the Germans expressed little interest in bombing the Spanish Republic to induce terror. As a senior Condor Legion officer put it, 'It would have been simple for the Nationalist Air Force to bomb Valencia, Barcelona or Madrid into ashes with incendiary bombs, but politically that was unacceptable . . . What would be the purpose of destroying the valuable industries of Bilbao or the weapons factory in Reinosa if they would be occupied in a short time? . . . Fighting in one's own land is a two-edged sword.' The Condor Legion found it could put its aircraft to their best use by interdicting Republican supply lines, attacking shipping and port facilities, and flying in direct support of the Nationalist army as it did in northern Spain."[2]

Contrary to what Corum said, the Luftwaffe did not have the capacity to destroy a city of the dimensions of Madrid, Barcelona, or Valencia. In fact, no air force would have had such capacity until years later, when the atomic bombs hit Hiroshima and Nagasaki. But even though it would not have been simple or even possible to completely destroy a city of these dimensions in 1936 or 1937, Corum was also wrong in stating that the destruction of "the valuable industries of Bilbao" had no purpose. But according to General Mola, the destruction of Basque industry did indeed serve a political purpose, and Richthofen wrote it down in his diary, a document that Corum knew and had studied in detail when writing his biography. Specifically, on April 2, 1937, General Mola explained to Richthofen in the course of a bitter discussion about the details of the campaign in the Basque Country that war was not as Richthofen saw it, that its goal was to destroy all the Basque – as well as Catalan – industry in order to rural-ize or impoverish these two nations. According to Mola, the Spanish state was dominated "in a completely unhealthy way" by Basque and the Catalan industry and, consequently, that industry had to be destroyed in order to put an end to the Basque and Catalan nationalism and "sanitize Spain."[3]

Corum has also written that "Wolfram von Richthofen was not a master of 'terror bombing' and never made city bombing his primary operational method. When he bombed towns and cities, he did it for justifiable tactical and operational reasons. His manner was ruthless, and he never expressed any moral qualms about his actions, nor did he show any sympathy for the people he bombed. His actions were part of a carefully calculated ruthlessness that one accepts in warfare."[4] I do not agree with the use of the term "justifiable" to refer to the bombing of cities and the consequent loss of human lives, and I do not agree that in war a "carefully calculated cruelty" must be accepted.

But, beyond these opinions, Corum asserted that Richthofen "made a few laconic remarks, and none of them referred to any success in ter-rorizing the Basques."[5] This is not so. Richthofen did mention the value of bombing to break the morale of the enemy. Specifically, on the very first day of the offensive in the Basque Country, he made reference in his diary to the significant effect of the cannonade of the artillery on morale, something about which he had already thought and by which he was not surprised.[6] Richthofen also referred in his diary to the "morale drive" that the bombings exerted on the own forces on April 26, the same day that Gernika was bombed.[7] But, fundamentally, when considering the war in the Basque Country, Richthofen stated objectively that the effect of the bombings on morale had been one of the most powerful weapons in his hands:

> We have forced the Reds to retreat step by step, with serious losses in staff and morale, and little material damage. The Red stands and defends himself tenaciously; we must fight at every step we advance. Since some troops only advance when the enemy does not fire, and the Spanish artillery always arrives too late and unprepared when the time comes to completely annihilate the enemy, the whole weight of the struggle falls on the air force, which destroys the enemy's morale

in the first place and only later produces casualties, pursuing the enemy and taking away their impetus.[8]

Richthofen concluded by saying that this task of breaking the morale of the enemy was only possible "because the enemy lacks an air force."[9]

Richthofen also insisted on the "very great" effect that the 100 and 250 kilo bombs had on their victims' morale in his report on *The Effect of the Bombing on Spanish Cities on the Vizcaya Front* of May 28, 1937.[10]

Richthofen was not alone in his assessment of the bombings' effect on morale. One would have been very blind not to realize it. In fact, the Spanish air command realized very early on the ineffectiveness or low tactical efficiency of the aerial bombings versus the great psychological impact that could be obtained from them. General Ettore Bastico, commander-in-chief of the Italian forces, informed Count Ciano in Rome on April 13, 1937, that the action of the aviation on the defenses of Bilbao was of "very little material value" and, concluded, as Richthofen did, that the use of artillery was also ineffective. Bastico added about the prisoners of war – whom they had obviously interrogated in this regard – that the air force's main value lay in the psychological effect it could exert on enemy troops, that is, in the "azione morale dell'aviazione"; he concluded categorically that the capture of Bilbao was going to be "difficult and very hard if the morale of the enemy is not broken."[11] General Velardi wrote in his report on April 13 that "the morale effect has proved even greater."[12] Mussolini was of the same opinion and, in a telegram to Bastico signed on June 21, 1937, he ordered him not to allow any truce with the enemy, who had to be "demoralized."[13]

If the bombing was a simple tactical or strategic operation, why did Franco order the proclamation of a lie? Moreover, why did he order the closing of the town, the removal of all evidence of the bombing, including corpses, and denial of the facts? It should also be asked why Ehrhart K. Dellmensingen, commander of the third Junkers Ju 52 bomber squadron that attacked Gernika, was required to write a flight report stating that he had thrown his cargo onto the Errenteria bridge, when he had not done so. Finally, it should be explained why the official version of the dictatorship for four decades was that Gernika had been set on fire by the Reds. And, regardless of the motivation and nature of the attack, bombing and strafing a population for three and a half hours on a market day, in which there were three military hospitals and between 10,000 and 12,000 civilians in an area of less than one kilometer,[2] in order to destroy "a bridge", is an atrocity. Launching the bombs on the urban center when – allegedly – there was no visibility, also demonstrated serious irresponsibility and a great lack of professionalism.

As Richthofen himself expressed with his usual sense of irony in a letter signed on May 25, 1937, "In Guernica, despite everything, I conducted myself very impolitely, of course!"[14]

Chapter 12

The destruction was mainly due to mismanagement of the Basque firefighters

The authors of the Machimbarrena Report asserted that, after light bombing, Gernika had "suffered a lot of damage," but "it had not been destroyed." They explained that a single bombing could have not caused the level of destruction registered in Gernika, which they instead attributed to arson by the "Reds." This was also one of the conclusions of the Herrán Report, which, concerning the above, added that the Basque soldiers and volunteers who were in Gernika that night looted the town. Jesus Obieta, 30 years of age, who was in the Talleres de Guernica shelter during the bombing, testified: "While the fire was raging the Red Separationists only occupied themselves with looting, carrying off their booty in lorries, including a portion of his stock of textile merchandise."[1] Julián Madariaga, 55, said that "these belongings were looted by the Reds, particularly the merchandise owned by the witness. He did not see militiamen in the town at the time of the bombing, but that they appeared afterwards, from which he deduces that they knew what was about to happen."[2]

José Fernandez, 47, testified: "The Reds made no protest against the bombing. On the contrary, they accused of being 'Fascists' those who, like Don Santos Uribe, merchant of Guernica and at present residing in Forua, endeavoured to extinguish the blaze in his house and in those of his neighbours."[3] Carmen Iturriarte, 27, also testified that "no steps were taken by the militiamen or firemen to prevent it, but that on the contrary, they employed themselves in looting [. . .]. her family had commented among themselves on the fact that the janitor of the *'batsoqui'* (house) [local Basque Nationalist Party headquarters] had left at six o'clock in the morning with a little bag full of silver."[4]

Rodolfo Basañez also lied when he said that "at eleven o'clock on the night of that same day a group of railway employees who belonged to the Reds searched the station, its offices and the house of the deponent, carrying off the official papers and a bundle which he supposes was the cash. At that hour there was no sign of fire in the station buildings which stand alone at least fifty feet away from any others and his statement is confirmed by the above-mentioned railway employees. At half-past eleven of the same night were seen flames which began to destroy the station building. [. . .] He considers that certain railway employees of Red sympathies who searched the station and carried off the official papers and the cash thereafter set fire to the station building and to his house. In addition, no attempt was made to check the flames."[5]

The authors of the Herrán Report blamed the firefighters not only for not having been able to do their job, but also for having helped spread the fire:

About half-past nine or ten o'clock at night they heard news which gave them some hope. Three fire-engines with their crews and equipment had arrived from Bilbao. All the townsfolk hurried to help to extinguish the blaze, and at last it was possible to couple up three hoses, which began to function. A little later, for no known reason, the pumps ceased to work. It was now about eleven at night, and very soon afterwards various official motor-cars made their appearance. In these were certain members of the Basque Government, and in another car three Englishmen who appeared to be newspapermen. From that time on, the firemen ceased to work, and prevented the townsfolk from making any use of the fire-engines. At eleven o'clock at night the railway station and the stationmaster's house adjoining was sacked [sic] and burned by the Reds. This building stood alone, as can be seen in the photograph No. 8 [included in the report]. The Reds also burned certain trucks . . . A little later one Pedro Olivares was successful in running up a hose for the purpose of putting out the blaze in his own house, but the firemen prevented him from working the pumps. He even offered them 500 pesetas to do the work, but they refused the money and pursued their obstructive tactics. The three Englishmen then offered to take Olivares to Bilbao in their car, as they wished him to give an account there of the burning of Guernica. One townsman, who was watching the oncoming flames, stoically proposed to the militiamen that they should plant a cannon in front of his house and blow it to pieces, in order that the gap thereby produced might check the conflagration, but his generous offer was not accepted. The fire continued all through the night of Monday the 26th April, and all Tuesday and Wednesday as well. On the Wednesday, three days after the fire had started, certain houses, which had not hitherto been involved, caught fire.[6]

Paraphrasing the Herrán Report, Jesús Salas stated that the troops in Gernika, either on a leave or at rest, did not help in the relief work and firefighting effort. He concluded that the destruction of Gernika was largely due to the ineffectiveness of the firemen of Bilbao, who "were notified very late, did not arrive until after 10 p.m. and left at three in the morning, without adopting measures appropriate to the magnitude of the fire."[7] He also observed that "no one believes that the village would have been saved with a more energetic response, but the percentages of buildings destroyed and seriously damaged could have been reduced and the subsequent fires of the days 27, 28 and 29 avoided."[8]

This was also the version told by Ferdinando Raffaelli, commander of the Italian bombing squadrons that attacked Gernika on April 26:

> The German air bombardment was certainly well 'focused' on the 'town' target, but the appearance of those walls in ruins on the ground and the almost total absence of craters on uncovered surfaces left many doubts about the true nature of these explosions. We could not exclude the hypothesis that after the already severe destructions caused by the German bombing that occurred on April 26, other hands had mined what remained standing to give a final touch to the propagandistic and theatrical presentation of a ruthlessly destroyed city, as well as the deaths of many inhabitants, in virtue of the cruel and absolutely unnecessary fury of the new barbarians. This assumption is also supported by the fact that Guernica was mainly a place for miners, people very familiar with the use and choice of explosives.[9]

But Gernika has never been a mining center, and Raffaelli fails to mention the participation of Italian air units.

Hermann Göring gave a similar account during the Nuremberg trials when he blamed Dutch firefighters' inappropriate action for the destruction of Rotterdam. Like the complainants of the Herrán Report, Göring said that "the great destruction was not caused by bombs but, as has been said, by fire. That can best be gleaned from the fact that all the buildings that were built of stone and concrete are still standing in the ruined part, while the older houses were destroyed. The spread of this fire was caused by the combustion of large quantities of fats and oils. Second – I want to emphasize this particularly – the spread of this fire could surely have been prevented by an energetic response on the part of the Rotterdam fire department, in spite of the coming storm."[10]

The Herrán Report's version of events is widely disproved by the dozens of oral testimonies of people who were in Gernika on the night of April 26 and the following days, as well as by abundant photographs and even video recordings showing Basque soldiers and firefighters trying to save the people who had been trapped under the ruins. Such is the case of those who were rescued from city council shelter whose entrance had been buried under the rubble. In short, there is no documentary evidence that anyone in Gernika spread the fires or looted anything. Not one of the 129 eyewitnesses that William Smallwood interviewed ever mentioned that anyone helped the spread of the fire or pillaged.[11] Indeed, blaming firefighters for the destruction of a town on which a minimum of between 20 and 29 tons of incendiary bombs were dropped is absurd, and by 7:40 p.m. on April 26 there was nothing to be looted in Gernika.

Chapter 13

Franco did not know anything

The first official version of the regime was that Gernika had not been bombed, so obviously Franco could not know that the town had been bombed; however, the second official version, that of the Machimbarrena and Herrán Reports, incorporated the idea of a minor bombardment and a subsequent destructive fire at the hands of the Basques themselves, the Asturians, the "expert dynamiters and arsonists accompanying the enemy hordes," or all of them acting at the same time. The problem with this second version was that someone should take responsibility for the bombing, and this someone was not going to be Franco.

Neither the Machimbarrena Report nor the Herrán Report made any reference to the order to bomb Gernika, but the authors of the latter indicated in their ninth conclusion that "the destruction of Guernica, therefore, cannot be attributed to German aircraft."[1] This reference to German aircraft is significant, especially considering that the regime's press had asserted that "there is no German or foreign aviation in National Spain. There is Spanish aviation, noble and heroic Spanish aviation,"[2] and that General Mola had sworn on his honor that he would surrender unconditionally to General José Miaja if someone showed that there were German volunteers in the national Army.[3]

The references to German aircraft did not escape the notice of the German Foreign Ministry and the Secretary of State for Foreign Affairs Hans Georg von Mackensen, who wrote a telegram to his embassy in Salamanca on May 4 protesting that the order given by Franco to deny the bombing had not been complied with:

> The ambassador in London [Joachim von Ribbentrop] telegraphs: 'From various sides, the embassy receives writings that, ignoring the lie, blame the bombing of Guernica on German planes. In private conversations, Franco's lie has in this regard, as before, a role of special importance, which is interpreted here in the sense that Franco indirectly recognizes

that the attack was carried out by German aviators. The discussion in the House of Commons could be used as a basis to induce Franco now to make an energetic and very firm denial, which would end the play on words.' Please persuade Franco to make an immediate and vigorous denial. The press here has rejected the deceitful news of the British while taking advantage of the evidence that exists about the destruction of the city by the Bolsheviks.[4]

In any case, despite German protests, the best weapon of the Spanish propaganda media was to drop all responsibility on "German planes," since the British press itself and in particular the articles by Monks, Steer, Corman, Holme, and Watson had referred to German Junkers and Heinkel aircraft. And from this version comes the idea that Franco did not order the bombing but that the German forces did "acting on their own."

Spanish authors such as Ricardo de la Cierva, Jaime del Burgo,[5] José M. Martínez Bande,[6] Vicente Talón,[7] and Jesús Salas have defended this idea, which has also been discussed by German authors such as Müller,[8] Galland,[9] and Jaenecke.[10] Corum did not participate in this hypothesis when he affirmed that the bombing of Gernika was carried out with the full approval of General Mola and his personnel.[11] De la Cierva wrote that "naturally, the generic responsibility of everything that happens in a war falls on those who direct it; and it would be absurd to exempt General Franco from responsibility for the bombing of Guernica, carried out by airplanes that had their base in the territory controlled by him and that theoretically were at his command. But Franco did not give the order to bomb Guernica; the operation was a German initiative and its direct responsibility falls on the commanders of the Condor Legion who used the sacred city of the Basques – also of the Basques fighting in Franco's army – as a test bed for experiences of total war."[12]

Salas stated that "only three people had the authority to order the bombing: Generals Mola and Sperrle, because of their respective positions as heads of the Northern Army and the air force operating in the Basque Country, and Lieutenant Colonel von Richthofen, by delegation of the head of the Condor Legion."[13] But this is not true. In fact, the General Instructions for Liaison with the Air Force of November 17, 1936, established that remote bombardments on localities could only be ordered by the superior command, that is, by Franco.[14] Mola and Sperrle could "request" towns be bombed, but only the General Headquarters had the power to issue the order. From this it is deduced that Franco gave the order to bomb Gernika and each and every one of the towns that were bombed in the course of the war.

On the other hand, Salas affirmed in another section of his book that, on January 5, General Sperrle requested permission to bomb Bilbao, and "Franco himself verbally denied permission and subsequently gave instructions to the Air Force Command to send a telegram to the Condor Legion that began by saying that 'without any express order, no city or city center will be bombed.'"[15]

Richthofen agreed with Colonel Juan Vigón, chief of staff of the Navarrese brigades, on the Supuestos de acción de la Legión Cóndor [Action plans of the Condor Legion] on the Basque front at the end of March 1937, before beginning the campaign. By virtue of these and the aforementioned General Instructions for Liaison with the Air Force, it was decided that the German units would always act in coordination with and under the command of Spanish officers who would plan the maneuvers and transmit their orders. Richthofen and Vigón would study these orders every morning before 8 a.m. and would make the necessary adjustments depending on the time and situation of the forces in the theater of operations.

Day after day Franco and Mola, with the knowledge of General Kindelán, chief in command of the rebel air force, transmitted orders concerning the actions of the air units that Vigón and Richthofen had to execute on the ground. This was done throughout the campaign and also on April 26 when the latter met in Bergara at 7 a.m. to review operations orders. The telegram from the General Headquarters of Salamanca to General Sperrle of May 7, 1937, states that "first line units [the Spanish command] directly requested aerial bombing of crossroads, executed by German and Italian air units."[16] And Richthofen himself reminded General Kindelán on August 9, 1937, that it was the Spanish command that ordered the bombing.[17]

As Angel Viñas pointed out, the first two paragraphs of this letter were adulterated when translated from the original German into Spanish. The original letter says that "the situation on land in the Vizcaya front on April 26, 1937, which led the command of the Army of the North to order an aerial bombardment of the bridge next to Gernika by the east was the following . . . ." But the Air Force Command translated the paragraph thus: "The situation of the troops on the Vizcaya front on April 26, 1937, to which the air attack was subordinated, was as follows. . . ."[18] It is obvious that the translation was falsified with the intention of eliminating from the text any reference to the Army of the North's command, that is, to Generals Mola and Franco.

Some authors have stated that Franco's General Headquarters did not order the bombing because there is no written copy of the order signed by Franco or Mola. De la Cierva said that "surely the most searched document in all the archives about the war in Spain is one in which Franco's order about Guernica is somehow reflected. Such a document has never been found simply because it does not exist."[19] And it certainly does not exist. But that does not mean that they did not know about this order or that they had not received it, since there is hardly any bombing order signed by Franco or Mola. In fact, there is no bombing order signed by any of the commanders who conducted the operations, whether they were Spanish, German, or Italian, and certainly it should not be inferred that nobody ordered the bombings or that no one knew anything about them, especially in the case of Gernika, where 20 percent of the planes available to Franco in the whole of the Iberian Peninsula were involved in a three-and-a-half-hour operation.

No officer wanted to sign these kinds of orders. Richthofen wrote in his diary that when on April 2 Mola gave the order to bomb the Galdakao gunpowder factory, he asked him to pass the order in writing. Mola passed the order, but without signing it, with the acronym "P.O." (by order). Richthofen then demanded that the order be signed and that Mola sign it.[20] On that occasion Mola had to comply, and he did send the bombing order signed in his own handwriting. Days later, the factory was bombed, but this was probably the only bombing order signed by the head of the Army of the North or by any other commander during the campaign in the Basque Country, where more than 1,100 bombing operations were carried out between July 1936 and August 1937.

Chapter 14

Spanish aircraft did not participate in the bombing

De la Cierva was exhaustive when stating that "it is thus proven that Guernica was bombed by [the] German-Italian air force on April 26, 1937."[1] Salas[2] and Talón[3] also asserted that the air units of the Northern Air Forces (FAN), Spanish aviation, did not participate in the bombing of Gernika.

However, the Summary of Operations of April 26, 1937, No. 211 of the Salamanca Air Command states: "Vitoria. The Breguet and the Heinkel 45, a service to the bridge of Guernica."[4] The squadrons of Breguet Br.19 of the FAN stationed at the aerodromes of Lasarte and Gasteiz were the 1-G-10 and the 2-G-10 that had about nine Breguet Br.19s, in addition to other types of airplane. The Heinkel He 45s were part of the squadrons 2-E-10, 3-E-10, and 4-E-10 that operated abundantly in the Basque Country.

The Summary of Operations is not equivocal and, although it is true that the Summary of Operations for April 26, 1937, of the FAN does not mention the attack of its units on Gernika, nor does it refer to the activity of the squadrons 1-G-10 and 2-G-10. According to this Summary of Operations, squads 1-G-15, 2-E-10, and 4-E-10 attacked the roads "that start from Durango," certain positions on Mount Urko, and a forest in the surroundings of Markina.

There is therefore no conclusive reason to deny the veracity of the document of Salamanca Air Command, since there is no material evidence that the Salamanca part is erroneous or that the part of the FAN is incomplete. Notwithstanding all this, under the heading "Error on the Salamanca report. The Spanish Aviation did not intervene," Salas concluded without any evidence that "in any case, the fact that some Heinkel 45s flew over Guernica does not alter the conclusions of our study, since if they did it went unnoticed by the people in Guernica.

Their small number and their light load of bombs make their possible presence little more than anecdotal."[5] But this is not true either. The Breguet Br.19 reconnaissance variant could load twelve 10-kilo bombs and, in fact, on April 25, one day before the bombing of Gernika, a Breguet Br.19 launched twelve A-5 or 150-kilo explosive bombs on its target at the Basque front. But the bombing variant of the Breguet Br.19 could carry up to 472 kilos of bombs under the fuselage or in a vertical pump hold prepared to load small bombs of up to 50 kilos.

Apart from the fact that, as the documentary evidence available to us indicates, some FAN aircraft may have attacked Gernika, the Lasarte and Gasteiz units did participate actively in the bombing by means of information services and aerial photography. Specifically, the photographs taken of Gernika on April 28 after the bombing by the Breguet Br.19s of the FAN are now available to the public in the Iglesias Brage Fund (Head of Operations of the Northern Front) of the Archive of the Kingdom of Galicia, in A Coruña. And it is necessary to emphasize that, to this day, I have not found any mention of this aerial activity in any of the 35 archives in which I have searched, among them that of Villaviciosa de Odón, where the Air Force records are deposited.

Chapter 15

It was an accident

Some authors have defended the bombing as "a lamentable error of calculation" due to technical limitations – that is, because the aircraft did not have the accurate means of bomb aim. This idea seems to originate with Adolf Galland, who noted that "the attack was verified under poor conditions of visibility, with primitive pointing devices."[1]

The Herrán Report pointed out that it would have been very difficult to destroy "the public sewer system" by means of an aerial bombing given the technical limitations of the airplanes of the time. According to this report, the Reds had placed explosive charges in the public sewage system, which explained why part of the drainage system was unusable. Without providing reliable data on the alleged damage, the authors expressed their doubts about the accuracy of the bombings, which could not have caused such damage: "Is it possible for an aviator to drop his bomb exactly in one place of the town through which the sewer line runs and repeat this indefinitely and always with the same success, while protecting themselves from attack from the ground and keeping an eye on its targets amidst the smoke produced by the explosions?"[2]

To this day, Corum has adopted this theory of the error of bombing, stating:

> Guernica was carpet bombed not because of any specific plan of the Germans to inflict terror, but because the German bombers of early 1937 had poor bombsights and were simply incapable of hitting precise targets. The German operational rationale for bombing towns like Guernica is outlined in a Condor Legion report to Berlin made on 11 February 1938: 'We have notable results in hitting targets near the front, especially in bombing villages which hold enemy reserves and headquarters. We have had great success because these targets are easy to find and can be thoroughly destroyed by carpet bombing.' In the report, it

was noted that attacks on point targets, such as bridges, roads, and rail lines, were more difficult and generally less successful.'[3]

But Corum failed to mention that incendiary bombs were used and the population was machine-gunned, facts certainly difficult to explain in terms of an "objective" such as the Errenteria bridge or a road junction. Corum also failed to mention that Richthofen ordered boxes loaded with incendiary bombs to be transported in the inner corridor of the Junkers Ju 52 and to be thrown by hand over Gernika, something that obviously would hinder the precision of the drop and that would not have been done if the objective would have been, in effect, the bridge of Errenteria. And Corum also failed to explain why Richthofen and Jaenecke described the attack as a great success despite having thrown between 31 and 46 tons of bombs without having even touched the bridge and having failed to stop the withdrawal of the Basque troops or to capture these troops. Additionally, Colonel Wilhelm Meise[4] considered the bombing of Gernika a great achievement of the Luftwaffe, and Jaenecke, who coordinated the activity of the Condor Legion and the Legionary Aviazione under Richthofen's orders in connection with the bombing of Gernika, described it as a "resounding success of the German air weapon."[5] But, fundamentally, Corum did not account for Richthofen's decision not to use the four Henschel Hs 123 dive-bombing aircraft available at the aerodrome of Gasteiz, just a few minutes flight from Gernika, designed specifically to destroy targets such as bridges. These were the only bombers stationed on the northern front that Richthofen did not use in the attack on Gernika on April 26.

Müller went further and affirmed that "the attacks carried out by the horizontal flight bombers, even when directed against major military targets, missed the target 90 percent of the time."[6] But, apart from all the incongruities noted above, the statements about the technical limitations of aviation at that time are contradicted by the facts and by Richthofen's references emphasizing the effectiveness of the bombing units that he led. Richthofen's diary is full of details on the accuracy levels of his air units, both on static targets and even on mobile targets, such as ammunition or ground transport trucks, which were destroyed by ground-attack aircraft on many occasions. In the case of Otxandio, Richthofen noted, after studying the ruins of the town, "I went to Ochandiano. Great effects of the bombing and the fighters of the A/88 [Heinkel He 70 reconnaissance aircraft squad]. Everywhere dead and mutilated, heavy trucks, which carried part of their ammunition, were destroyed."[7] Richthofen also wrote that the effect of the bombings on the structures of the houses in the course of the bombings of Durango, Eibar, and Gernika had been very satisfactory, with a large number of demolished houses and a large percentage of these localities ruined. Specifically, in reference to the bombing of Eibar, Richthofen wrote that "the repeated attacks from a height of only 600 to 800 meters, which was possible in virtue of the absence of any type of anti-aircraft or ground defense, also provided good results here. They were favored by the Italian launching system and the degree of destruction reached 60 percent."[8]

There are many authors who, together with the aforementioned pilots Cenarrusa and Robinson, talk about precision in the shooting ability of the Henschel Hs 123 dive bombers, which would have been perfect to destroy a target such as the Errenteria bridge. Authors such as Peter C. Smith,[9] John Weal,[10] Nigel Askey,[11] Jean D. Lepage,[12] and Dennis Showalter[13] have underlined the level of accuracy of the Henschel Hs 123 dive bombers, which they have defined as "absolutely accurate" (pinpoint accuracy).

As Corum has pointed out, Richthofen's priority objective during the Polish campaign was the transport system, and the two air fleets at his disposal, equipped with Henschel Hs 123 and Junkers Ju 87, "struck numerous major rail junctions and rail bridges throughout Poland."[14] Specifically, in the course of the Polish offensive on the Bzura River on September 11, 1939, Richthofen launched various Henschel Hs 123 squadrons on the Polish forces, which were decimated, and the river bridge at the height of Witkowice was destroyed.[15] It is even more surprising that Corum, who underlines in Gernika's case the inefficient bomb-dropping systems of the German planes, which were "incapable of hitting precise targets," affirms that these same aircraft had a high precision of shooting in the course of the Polish campaign where, according to his own words, "[t]he Polish transport: system had been paralyzed by air strikes; bridges were destroyed, and several trains, including one of the Polish army's armored trains, were smashed by Stukas. On 3 September van Richthofen's airmen shattered an entire Polish cavalry brigade with repeated attacks. Whenever a good target was identified, von Richthofen would order an attack – usually in group strength (thirty to forty Stukas or Henschel 123s)."[16] The examples of the effective use of the Henschel are numerous. During the Belgian campaign, Richthofen intensively used the Henschel Hs 123 squadron

II/LG2 units, which provided air support to ground troops, pushing back the Second Grenadier Company, which lost 216 men in a single action.[17] On May 21, 1940, a Henschel Hs 123 squadron destroyed about forty French tanks, on the move, in the vicinity of Cambrai.[18]

Strangely, none of the above-mentioned authors indicated that the "error in the shooting" resulted in the complete demolition of 85.22 percent of all buildings in the town and the ruin of 99 percent of Gernika. To paraphrase Pete Cenarrusa, throwing between 31 and 46 tons of bombs on a target and not hitting it is as much as affirming that they were utterly incompetent pilots, too inept to be minimally credible.[19]

Other authors have referred to an accident but resorted to the idea that the smoke obfuscated the view of the target. Franco himself, in a telegram sent to General Sperrle on May 7, 1937, wrote that the German and Italian air units' actions "[affected] the town due to a lack of visibility [created by the] smoke and the clouds of dust [produced by the] bombs [dropped from the] airplanes."[20]

Richthofen was also one of the first to circulate this version of events in a letter to General Kindelán, in which he stated that the bombing took place under conditions of poor visibility. According to Richthofen, the attack of the three aircraft of Lieutenant Moreau's experimental bombing squad caused such smoke that the observers of the Junkers Ju 52 bombers later saw that Gernika was burning with great intensity at different points. As a result, when the bulk of the Junkers formation bombed Gernika "it was quite difficult to observe the targets from above" because of smoke and "nobody could recognize the targets such as roads, bridges and the suburbs, and bombed the center" of the village, which in turn would explain why they did not destroy the bridge.[21] The report of the Scientific Section of the Luftwaffe offers the same explanation: "vision was totally insufficient, because the city was immersed in flames and smoke."[22]

Contradicting Richthofen, who pointed out that the smoke was created by Moreau's squadron, Lieutenant Hans von Beust, head of the second bombing squad of K/88 of Junkers Ju 52 that attacked Gernika, stated in 1973 that it was the discharge of the first Junkers Ju 52 K/88 squadron that "produced a huge amount of dust and smoke, the terrain that spanned the bridge and the city completely escaped the vision [of the pilots], so that the next two attack squads could only throw their bombs by approach. Because of this, and due to a strong drift of the wind, the mass of the bombs fell on the city."[23] And furthermore the pilot added that "given the weather conditions and the release of dust and smoke", the city was seriously affected, unintentionally, by the bombs. The image that I saw during the flyby is still clear before my eyes."[24] Beust never explained why, given that he could not see the target during his first pass given the large amount of smoke, he could see it so clearly in the second.

Ehrhart K. Dellmensingen, commander of the third squadron of Junkers Ju 52 bombers that attacked Gernika, also explained in 1983: "When I arrived at Guernica it was totally burning. I partially saw the first two squadrons and their bombs, almost always west of the eastern edge of the town. An east wind blew . . . and the bombs of my squadron also fell there, even though they had made the approach with a wide correction on the target to the west. The firebombs blazed above the smoke field, so it could be said that they had fallen on the village. [Mayor Robert] Fuchs asked that I write a deceptive report: that we had not droppedall the bombs on the city. I did not want to accept this report and wanted it to be modified. I rejected this emphatically, in the presence of Seppi Kögl, assistant of the group."[25]

And historiography has reproduced this version. Salas, following the testimonies of the German pilots, stated that smoke caused by the bombs of the first squadron of Junkers Ju 52 led by Karl von Knauer, which completely covered the targets, prevented the second squadron led by Hans von Beust and the third led by Ehrhart K. Dellmensingen from correctly calculating the drop and, as a consequence, they were forced to drop the load blindly, and missed.[26] Müller also stated that "fearing that the roads were full of enemy troops, the bombers flew at a high altitude, losing accuracy of their attack what they gained in security. The release of smoke and the action of the wind prevented the planes from enhancing the launching of their load."[27]

Captain Stefano Castellani, who led the Italian bombing squadron No. 280, wrote that, starting from Soria, they arrived over the Gernika valley at "4:25 p.m., at which time we turned south towards the mouth of the river. The visibility was optimal. Shortly before launching, we spotted an unknown plane under us that was heading in the opposite direction of ours. Soon after, he turned away. We dropped the bombs at 16:30."[28] This version belies all others. As we will see, Castellani also lied in his report on the performance of his squad, but the plane he saw flying under his Savoia-Marchetti SM.79 had to be one of the aircraft of

Moreau's experimental unit returning to their air base in Burgos after having bombed Gernika, since these were the only bombers that acted before 4:30 that afternoon. It follows that the bombing of Moreau's squadron did not cause as much smoke as Richthofen intended to make people believe, since he writes that after he dropped his load on Gernika, "the visibility was optimal."

Flying low and slow and under no pressure, since there were no anti-aircraft batteries, the aerial photographs of the operation confirm that the bombing of Gernika was surgical. If we look at the train track, we see that on one side, where the railway station is located, the destruction was total, with a result of 100 percent of the buildings completely demolished. However, just in front of the station, on the other side of the train track, just 20 meters away, the buildings of the industrial sector are perfectly intact, with hardly any damage. And this fact is perceptible throughout the nearly 1,000 meters of track from the Errenteria bridge to the last buildings of the industrial sector, south of the town. The same can be seen north of the town, where the streets of San Juan and Portu Kalea mark the limit between total destruction (to the south) and the area of the palaces on the way to Sukarrieta (north), which was not affected. Juan Calzada Street also served as a dividing line between both areas, the destroyed and the preserved. Twenty meters or even fewer between the total devastation and the unaffected zone is undoubtedly an achievement of precision and accuracy in the bomb drop. Without a doubt it was for this reason that both Jaenecke and Richthofen referred to the bombing in terms of a "great success" and went to play cards along with Sperrle on the beach in Zarautz.

Neither the bridge nor the weapons factory was bombed because they were was not supposed to be bombed. As a 10-year-old witness of the bombing of Gernika put it, during a German bombing, weapons factories were much safer places than hospitals.[29]

Chapter 16

Richthofen ordered his men to spare Gernika and to throw bombs as a signal

The German, Italian, and Spanish commanders strove to express their reverence for human life and values and insisted on the fact that their respective air forces had strict orders to respect civilian populations and city centers. Indeed, the report of the Scientific Section of the Luftwaffe stressed that pilots of the Condor Legion had strict orders not to harm civilians: "All aviators, following orders, had nevertheless respected the place. Rather, it was turned into a pile of ruins by the Reds, according to a plan of fires and blowing [up]."[1] The order of attack of the Italian units reads similarly, stating that the objective is the Errenteria bridge and literally emphasizing that "the town, for obvious political reasons, should not be bombed."[2]

It is difficult to find examples of bombing orders in which the need to respect a town is stressed so strongly, especially in the context of Nazi Germany and Fascist Italy. Also suspicious is the reference to the *"evidenti ragioni politiche"* not to bomb Gernika, since before April 26, 1937; no one could know that the bombing of Gernika was going to become headline news in the European and American press. On the other hand, in open contradiction to the order, the bombs were dropped on the train station, on the church of San Juan, and in the middle of the city center, according to a large number of witnesses of the bombing.[3]

The regime-controlled press and radio in Spain also argued that Gernika had been spared: "We have not only respected Guernica for being Guernica. We have respected it, Basques of good faith, as we respect everything that is and shall be forever Spanish, within a very short time, the only and true Spain."[4] Salas wrote that "the permanent attitude of Franco's General Headquarters relating to the bombings of city centers throughout 1937 and 1938 was to avoid it" and gave an example of that. According to the author, when on January 5 General Sperrle requested permission to bomb Bilbao in retaliation for the lynching and death of prisoners in several prisons in the city, Franco refused to do so and gave precise instructions underlining that without his express order Sperrle should not bomb any city. He added that the Condor Legion should be careful when bombing in order to avoid innocent victims.[5]

However, none of the pilots was ever sanctioned because of "an error" that encompassed the complete destruction of the town and the deaths of more than 2,000 people. Even stranger, Franco demanded that "precision was required" when – as we have seen in previous chapters – Salas himself and many other authors have stressed that it was practically impossible to bomb accurately. But, fundamentally, what is really surprising is that Franco's instructions were ignored. Because the fact is that between January 6 (one day after having completed those instructions) and April 26, 1937, at least 226 bombing operations were registered on Basque soil, most of them against city centers. Virtually all towns in Bizkaia were bombed, repeatedly, during the spring campaign of 1937.[6]

Richthofen even wrote that incendiary bombs were dropped not to harm Gernika or its inhabitants, but rather by way of a signal, in order to indicate to the infantry the termination of the bombing, so that they could advance on the town and capture it.[7] He also stated that he ordered the three rapid bombers of Moreau's squadron to fly over Gernika for a long time "at medium heights" to "alert the residents," and that only later, when the residents had run to safety, did the aviators drop their bombs on the targets "with good enough aim"[8] – all 45 minutes before the general attack. Basically, Richthofen claimed that they were bombing to save lives.

All the above directly conflicts with the air command's decision at the start of the Basque campaign in relation to aerial attacks, which had three main goals: enemy positions, local reserves, and other sectors "without considering civilians."[9] It also conflicts with the reality of what happened during the bombing campaign, which resulted in the destruction of a large number of urban centers. Legutio and the greater Bilbao were bombed 56 times throughout the war in the Basque Country; Markina and Zornotza suffered 40 bombing operations; Zigoiti, 33; Mungia, 32; Bermeo, 29; Galdakao, 27; Eibar, Otxandio, and

Larrabetzu, 25; Irun and Leioa, 23; Barakaldo, Elorrio, and Lemoa, 22; Arrasate and the positions of their municipality in Santa Marina, Udala, and Kurtze Txiki 21; Donostia, Durango, and Sondika, 18 (in the case of Donostia, 8 of the bombings were naval); Lezama and Zeanuri, 15; Dima, Getxo, and Ubide, 14; Arrigorriaga Lekeitio, Ugao-Miravalles, and, Zuia 13; Abadiño, 12; the positions of Bergara, Ondarroa, Elgoibar, and Mañaria, 11; . . . the list is endless.[10]

Chapter 17

Nine, 39, or 43 aircraft participated in the bombing

Some authors have tried to reduce the number of airplanes in order to minimize the dimension and impact of the bombing.

One of the first narratives attempting to reduce the number of airplanes was the report of the Scientific Section of the Luftwaffe, which stressed that nine airplanes took part in the bombing.[1] Machimbarrena and Miláns del Bosch reported that a total of about eight or nine bombs were dropped, suggesting that the town was bombarded by a single squad of planes that launched between six and eight large-caliber explosive bombs. The Herrán Report did not offer any information about the number of airplanes involved in the bombing but tended to minimize their number by making repeated references to "several" airplanes. Carmen Iturriarte, one of the informants for the Herrán Report, said that around 5 p.m. groups of planes began arriving, of which she counted first five and then nine, some coming from the direction of Bermeo and others from Amorebieta, and that she did not know if they were German.[2] Luis Gómez also testified that around 4 p.m. he saw a group of planes headed to the sea, "two-engine in the first group and three-engine in the second."[3]

Lieutenant Karl von Knauer, commander of the first Junkers Ju 52 K/88 bombing squadron, said that "Moreau's squadron did not attack Guernica on April 26, 1937,"[4] but either he was wrong or he lied, because Richthofen himself referred to the participation of three of the aircraft of Moreau's squad in his diary.[5]

Salas listed 39 aircraft involved in the bombing: 3 Savoia-Marchetti SM.79s, 2 Heinkel He 111s, 1 Dornier Do 17, and 5 Fiat CR.32s during the first phase of the attack and then 19 Junkers Ju 52s, 5 Fiat Cr.32s, and 4 Messerschmitt Bf.109s. However, Salas did not include the twelve planes of the first Heinkel He 51 squadron led by Harro Harder, arguing that they did not attack the city center but rather the outskirts of Gernika and, with this same reasoning he excluded the five Fiat Cr.32s led by Corrado Ricci who, according to the official report, "made a flight over the Durango front," a flight of less than one minute from Gernika. In fact, these fighters' mission was to strafe the outskirts of Gernika in order to keep within the circle of fire all those who wanted to flee from the city center. And, in effect, when describing the bombing, Salas included Harder's and Ricci's squadrons, which would make for a total of 56 aircraft according to Salas's estimates.[6]

Corum wrote that 43 aircraft participated in the attack, but without explaining where he obtained this data or mentioning what type of aircraft they were.[7] Müller wrote without great precision that the bombing was executed "by a few dozen German and Italian planes."[8] Talón did not give a number but said that the figure given by the reporter George Steer "is not acceptable" since "the liquidation of a target of the characteristics of Guernica did not require them either."[9] It must be assumed that the "target" referred to by Talón is the Errenteria bridge, since in his book he defended the thesis that this was the main target of the attack. Indeed, the bridge would have only required a single dive-bomber, but Steer said that, according to witnesses, between 40 and 50 aircraft, including 10 fighters, participated in the bombing. The truth is that Steer's figure is very accurate, since today we have documented the participation of 59 or 63 planes, 32 of which were fighter aircraft.[10] To these we have to add the aircraft of the Spanish Air Force, whose number is unknown.

The participation of a greater number of aircraft has been documented. Lieutenant Hans von Beust, head of the second Junkers Ju 52 bombing squad, said that "we flew in four attack squads, six planes each,"[11] which makes a total of 24 Junkers Ju 52s. Talón said that the Legion Condor did not have "such a large number of aircraft" in 1937,[12] but he was wrong. By virtue of the report of General Pietro Pinna, the rebel aviation had 316 aircraft on April 17, 1937, and, according to the Condor Legion report of April 12, the German command had 35 bombers at war in the military arena, including 23 Junkers Ju 52s (two in Seville), 3 Junkers Ju 86s, 2 Dornier Do 17s (1 in Seville), 3 Heinkel He 111s, and 4 Henschel Hs 123s, as well as 26 fighters, 20 Heinkel He 51s and 6 Messerschmitt Bf.109s (5 in Seville) and 12 Heinkel He 70 spotter planes.[13]

In Gernika, the air command decided to use 20 percent of the rebel aviation available in the whole of the Iberian Peninsula for three and a half hours – a disproportionate figure indeed if the target was a 70-foot-long bridge.

Chapter 18

Eight or 28 tons of bombs were dropped

In the course of a bombardment, the level of material destruction and casualties is generally proportional to the number of aircraft involved, the tonnage of bombs dropped, and the bombing density (or the quotient between the total tonnage of bombs and the area where the bombs were released). Even the earliest reports attempted to reduce the tonnage of explosives dropped on Gernika.

The Scientific Section of the Luftwaffe was one of the first documents to reduce the number of bombs dropped, asserting that the attack on April 26 was executed by nine planes that dropped, "in a single flight," "nine 250-kilogram bombs and 114 50-kilogram ones, altogether 7,950 kilos" of explosive.[1] Apart from reducing the total tonnage by a factor of five, the Scientific Section lied by omission, not making reference to the incendiary bombs.

In a secret report of May 28, 1937, Colonel Joachim von Richthofen said that "31,000 kilos of bombs"[2] were dropped. This document is of vital importance because, although it is very possible that Richthofen was lying and that the total tonnage of bombs was higher than 40,000 kilos, it establishes without a doubt an absolute minimum of 31 tons. In any case, according to the colonel, "the insignificant number of bombs dropped inside the city cannot in any way have produced the level of destruction attained in the city."[3] Apparently, according to Richthofen, dropping between 31 and 46 tons of bombs in an area of less than one square kilometer^2 full of civilians was "insignificant."

Lieutenant Karl von Knauer, head of the first K/88 Junkers Ju 52 squadron, said that "the target was attacked in one pass with 50 kg bombs with delayed fuses (with short interval in [the] succession [of bombing waves])."[4] Knauer was lying; in fact, he lied a lot, and in general he did it quite badly. Referring to a single pass, and omitting the launching of incendiary bombs, and stating that only 50-kilo bombs were dropped (which are obviously less destructive than those of 250 kilos), he tried to reduce the impact that the bombing had on the town.

Corum, supported by no evidence and without mentioning the origin of his calculations, stated that "[o]n 26 April the Germans attacked the town with forty-three bombers and fighters and dropped approximately thirty-five tons of high-explosive bombs and incendiaries."[5] Ricardo de la Cierva, relying on a letter sent by Jesús Salas, said that the number of bombs dropped by the Savoia-Marchetti SM.79 on Gernika was "12 bombs of 12 kg per aircraft," that is, a total of 144 kilos per plane.[6] This assertion is totally illogical because if we take into account that each Savoia-Marchetti SM.79 could load up to 1,800 kilos of bombs, we must inquire why the air command would send three Savoias with the cargo that only one plane could have transported. But, in addition, Salas pointed out, on the same page of this same book, that these planes "dropped the 50 kg bombs on the targets," which obviously is in open contradiction with the above. De la Cierva also failed to mention the number of 50-kilogram bombs included in the official Italian report of 1937, which in turn is also false, as we shall see.

Salas wrote: "The Savoia-79, whose only objective was the Renteria bridge, carried 12 50-kg bombs by plane; the Italian Legionary Air Force had 500, 250 and 100 kg bombs, but the command at the Soria air base considered that [these planes] were not suitable for such a small target [as the Errenteria bridge] and preferred a greater number of bombs, albeit smaller ones, to increase the probability of impact, which, with the means of the time, was very small."[7] But this explanation is also biased. As Pete Cenarrusa explained, 12- or 50-kilogram bombs are not suitable for blowing up a bridge. The way to do it would have been with a single bomb of 250 kilos dropped by one of the four Henschel Hs 123 aircraft that Richthofen had in the aerodrome of Gasteiz – just a 20-minute flight from Gernika.

In general, Salas concluded that 28.22 tons of bombs were dropped in Gernika.[8] Given that the official reports of the Gernika operation of April 26 have disappeared, the only way to calculate the number of bombs and the total tonnage of explosives launched is by calculating the number of aircraft that participated in the bombing. Salas estimated that only 25 bombers participated (when today we have documented the participation of 27 or 30 bombers)[9] and, with no other criteria than his opinion, decided that they flew with half the cargo they could carry, or approximately 1,100 kilos per plane. But we know that in 1935 the Savoia-Marchetti SM.79 could load almost 2,000 kilos of explosives per plane, the Heinkel He 111 and the Junkers Ju 52 had the capacity to transport around 1,500 kilos of bombs, and the Dornier Do 17 of 1937 could carry around 1,000 kilos of explosive. As pilots Pete Cenarrusa and Williard Robinson pointed out, the only reason to reduce the load was to increase speed and maneuverability, which was important in the presence of enemy fighters or anti-aircraft batteries. But Richthofen knew that there were no enemy planes at the Basque front.

Moreover, Salas failed to mention in his chapter on the estimation of the total load of bombs that Richthofen ordered boxes of incendiary bombs to be loaded in the inner corridor of the Junkers Ju 52 to be thrown out by hand. Although the Junkers Ju 52 had the capacity to load 1,500 kilos of explosive in the bomb racks, they had a total load capacity of more than 3,000 kilos. And Richthofen took advantage of this. If the German colonel took the opportunity to introduce boxes inside, it would not have made any sense to load the magazines with just half of their capacity.

When I first calculated the total tonnage of bombs, I estimated an absolute minimum of 31 tons, which would be the amount if the 27 or 30 bombers flew with half the total possible load, something very unlikely, as we have seen. A year later, Angel Viñas gave me a copy of the secret report prepared by Richthofen on May 28, 1937, in which he figures the total tonnage in 31 tons, which is fully confirmed and documented in my calculation. However, the total amount should have been much higher, around 41 or even 46 tons of bombs,[10] and this calculation does not include the six 10-kilo bombs transported by each of the Heinkel He 51, which could make up to four trips to the air base of Gasteiz to refuel.

Nor is it true that the bombers made a single pass over Gernika. The bombs transported in the bomb holders could all be dropped on Gernika in a second, by means of a handle. At a cruise speed of something more than 200 km/h, bombers had 15 seconds of flight over the town, time enough to release the cargo in the bomb racks. However, a person could not throw more than three or four 25-kilo boxes of incendiary bombs from the inner corridor of the Junkers Ju 52 through the outside door, so they had to make two or even three passes over Gernika. Given they could not throw them all over the village, Basque soldier Martín M. Berreteaga recounts that they threw the ones that remained on the aircraft on Mount Urkiola and other places on their return to the Burgos aerodrome because bomber crews did not like landing with bombs on board; if they did not launch the incendiary bombs on their targets, they would drop them where they could.[11]

Chapter 19

Gernika was bombed at 1,500, 2,300, 3,500, 3,600, and 3,800 meters of altitude

Sometimes, in the presence of anti-aircraft batteries or enemy fighters, the bombers had to drop their cargo at high altitudes, beyond the reach of the mentioned batteries and above the flight height of the fighters. Naturally, the higher the flight height, the greater the error range, so to make credible the explanation that a calculation error caused Gernika's destruction. These false accounts invoked astronomical flight heights.

One of the first documents to refer to a fantastic flight height, the report of the Scientific Section of the Luftwaffe, specified that the town was bombed at 2,300 meters of altitude, in a single flight.[1] Lieutenant Hans von Beust, head of the second Junkers Ju 52 squadron, said they bombed "at an altitude of 3,500 meters or so."[2] Lieutenant Karl von Knauer, head of the first K/88 squad of Junkers Ju 52, said that "the altitude of the flight was 1,500 meters."[3] The report of Squadron No. 280 of the Aviazione Legionaria, written by Castellani, stated literally that "we released the cargo at 16:30 from a height of 3,600 meters. The shot is long, and we bombed, among other things, the railway station. A short time later, a thick stratum of clouds approached, which prevented us from observing the terrain in our flight back to Soria. After flying over the area again in windy weather, we landed without incident at 5:05 p.m."[4]

Based on this information, the historian Ferdinando Pedriali asserted emphatically that flying at this altitude, it would have been practically impossible to damage the bridge: "No! It was very difficult to hit the bridge, especially from a height of 3,600 meters. Even during World War II, when they had much more adequate devices, the Americans had a hard time destroying bridges. The bridges over the Po River were bombed hundreds of times before being destroyed."[5]

But the above is not completely correct. Although a bridge was not an easy target in 1937, it was not impossible to destroy a bridge from the air. We have referred to some of the bridges destroyed in the course of the war in the Basque Country, and hundreds more were bombed from the air between 1936 and 1945. Archival documentation supports the opinion of war pilots. Richthofen managed to fly over the Portugalete bridge, and we have aerial photographs of bridges destroyed by Italian aviation at the Archive of the Italian Air Force in Rome. In fact, as we have seen, not only were static targets such as bridges destroyed, but so were moving targets such as tanks hit by dive bombers of both parties at war, as in the course of the Battle of Guadalajara in March 1937.

It is not credible that the bombing was carried out at 3,600 meters of altitude when, as confirmed by the report prepared by Colonel Ferdinando Raffaelli, commander of the Soria bombing squads that Castellani led, the normal bombing height during a day attack was between 1,200 and 1,800 meters, as long as there were enemy fighters.[6] Moreover, even night bombings were carried out at a maximum height of 3,000 meters, according to Raffaelli. Once again, only in presence of heavy anti-aircraft battery fire or enemy planes was it advisable to bomb at 3,500 meters and, when there were high caliber anti-aircraft batteries, up to 4,000 or 4,500 meters, but neither of these conditions was met in Gernika.[7]

Two documents confirm categorically that Castellani, Beust, and Knauer lied. On the one hand, the Igeldo Meteorological Observatory's weather report indicates that at 12:00 hours on April 26 a north-north-east breeze of force 3, at 3.4 m/s was blowing, and two hours later a stratocumulus bank was generated at 900 meters of altitude and, on top of this, a second layer of clouds at 3,000 meters.[8] This confirms that no one could had bombed from more than 900 meters because, as observed by Junkers Ju 52 crew member Angel Seibane, the instruments of the time did not allow the dropping of bombs from above the clouds, much less over two banks of clouds, simply because it was impossible to see anything.[9]

In addition, Joachim von Richthofen asserted that Gernika was bombed at an altitude of between 600 and 800 meters, that is, from below the clouds.[10] It was not the first time; in Eibar, German and Italian bombers did the same thing when they bombed the city from

600 to 800 meters, which was possible given the absence of any type of anti-aircraft or ground defense.[11]

The absolute majority of the witnesses who saw the planes bomb Gernika confirm this. The Basque soldiers José R. Urtiaga and Antxon Zabalia, who were in Burgogana, a mountain 190 meters high east of Gernika, saw the first Heinkel He 51 that attacked Gernika launch the first bombs on the station flying "very low, below us."[12] Other soldiers, such as Pedro Gezuraga, Aurelio Artetxe, Iñaki Rezabal, and Faustino Pastor, stated the same.[13]

In spite of all this, Ricardo de la Cierva, based on the reproduction of an Italian document that Jesús Salas sent to him, stated in 2003 that the attack height of the Savoia-Marchetti SM.79 was 3,800 meters, although soon after he wrote that they had bombed from 3,600 meters.[14] And Salas himself took for granted the flying heights that the German and Italian pilots indicated, concluding that "all these technical inaccuracies made it very difficult to achieve specific targets."[15]

Lies generate problems of consistency. Pedriali insisted on highlighting the courage of the Italian pilots and the technical capacity of the Aviazione Legionaria, stating, for example, that "the aviators who went to Spain came largely from the Ethiopian campaign, but there were also others who came from very advanced aviation academies. They even admitted Germans as students. The fighter and bomber pilots sent to Spain were among the best."[16] However, immediately afterwards, he was forced to defend the thesis that, after throwing between 31 and 46 tons of bombs, they did not hit the target. Richthofen was not of the same opinion and, rightly or wrongly, pointed out on numerous occasions that the Italians were completely incompetent; the information available confirms that the rebel command was of the same opinion since, after the disaster of Guadalajara, Franco arranged for the Aviazione Legionaria to act on the northern front under the coordination of Richthofen, and this was arrangement until the Brunete offensive forced Franco to transfer his best air units, which apparently were not the Italians but rather the Condor Legion, to Madrid.

Chapter 20

Seventy-one percent of the city was destroyed

The Machimbarrena Report – prepared in a single afternoon, more specifically in two hours – introduced data relating to the percentage destruction of Gernika.

The Herrán Report's eleventh conclusion was that "[t]he fire and the explosions caused the total destruction of 71 percent of the houses in Guernica; 7 percent were damaged to a less but nevertheless noteworthy extent, and the remaining 22 percent were damaged slightly."[1] The Machimbarrena Report repeated the same idea, stressing that "Guernica possessed some 300 houses; of these 71 percent have been completely destroyed, and 7 percent have been badly battered about. The remaining 22 percent are damaged, but not to the same extent, and into these the population has crowded, with all the inconveniences which are to be expected in such circumstances."[2] In addition, they added in the third conclusion that no damage was caused to the Tree of Gernika, the Parliament House, the convents "converted into military barracks," or the arms and munitions factories."[3] In this case, the editors of the report were somehow trying to explain that the tree and the armament factories were not destroyed albeit that that "the Reds had burned the village down," but did not not want to destroy these things.

The Herrán commission based its eleventh conclusion on the testimony of 51-year-old Salustiano Olazabal, who stated that "of the approximate 300 houses which made up Guernica about 71 percent are destroyed, about 7 percent arc very seriously damaged, and the rest damaged, but not to the same extent."[4] In conclusion, of a total of approximately 300 buildings, 71 percent were completely destroyed (about 213), another 7 percent (about 21) seriously damaged and the remaining 22 percent (about 66) damaged in varying degrees.[5]

Several authors have echoed this information. Ricardo de la Cierva stated in 2003 that after the bombing "the fire spread to the city center and affected 70 percent of the houses of Guernica, although the historic Tree and the House of Parliament were unharmed."[6] Corum further reduced the level of destruction by claiming that the bombing only affected 50 percent of the town: "The attack leveled and burned about half of the town and killed approximately 300 people, mostly civilians."[7] Under the heading "Smoky ruins," Talón concluded that "the bombing had liquidated the old part of the town – the foundational part – as well as a series of constructions. As architect Cárdenas would establish at the end of the war, 721 houses were destroyed [it really meant 271 houses], which represents 71 percent of the total buildings were lost completely, while 7 percent suffered serious damage and only the rest were unscathed or with minor defects."[8]

Jesús Salas went somewhat further and, based on the population census of Bizkaia in 1930, added to the 318 buildings in Gernika those of the districts and towns of Lumo, Arana, San Pedro, and Zallo, and those of the Errenteria neighborhood, all of which makes a total of 492 buildings. Subsequently, given that the Herrán Report mentions that 271 houses were completely destroyed, Salas deduced illegitimately (and without mentioning that these 271 buildings were all located in the city center of Gernika) that the buildings destroyed in the bombing were 55 percent of the total buildings in the "Guernica urban grouping." And later he wrote that, "if we refer exclusively to the 364 buildings of the town of Guernica and the Renteria neighborhood, the proportion amounts to 74.4 percent, a value similar to that indicated by the industrial engineer Salustiano Olazabal Menárguez to the commission in charge of drafting the Herran Report: 71 percent of the buildings destroyed and 7 percent severely damaged."[9] These calculations are neither valid nor justifiable. In order to reduce the percentage of demolished buildings and to give legitimacy to the Herrán Report, Salas introduced into his calculation all buildings of the whole Urdaibai valley.

We have documentary evidence that the bombing caused the complete ruin of 85.22 percent of the buildings in Gernika and that affected the remaining 99 percent. That is, 85.22 percent of the buildings were literally demolished, and 99 percent were damaged, so that only one percent of the buildings in Gernika were unharmed. Specifically, contrary to what Talón said, Gonzalo Cárdenas, architect of the General Direction for Devastated Regions in charge of the reconstruction of Gernika, clearly indicated in his reconstruction project that out of the 318 buildings that were in Gernika in April 1937, 271 were "totally destroyed," meaning, mathematically, that the bombing completely destroyed 85.22 percent of the buildings in Gernika. Moreover, according to the data provided by Cárdenas, the 271 buildings totally destroyed by the bombing in Gernika represented 67.58 percent of the buildings totally destroyed in the whole of Bizkaia (excluding Bilbao), the reconstruction cost of which was of approximately 12 million pesetas, while the expenses for the whole of Bizkaia (excluding Bilbao) were about 35 million pesetas.[10]

Despite all this, several authors still repeat that the bombing destroyed 71 percent of the buildings or even that the bombing destroyed 71 percent of the town.

Chapter 21

Forty-five people died in the Andra Mari shelter

Joachim von Richthofen wrote in his diary four days after the bombing that "a small segment [of the population] perished in shelters that were hit."[1] Due to the strategy and logic underlying the bombing, some of the refuges proved to have been solidly built and withstood the explosion and the effect of the incendiary bombs, but others turned into deadly traps for those who sought shelter in them. The bombing was designed to catch victims within the fire perimeter of the city center, and was executed in four phases:

1. 4:20. A plane approached slowly from the east, from Mount Oiz, in order to be seen, and the bells of the church of Andra Mari rang, so people went to the shelters. This lonely Heinkel He 51 dropped six 10-kilo bombs on the city center.
   a. Around 4:25. The experimental bombardment squad led by Rudolf von Moreau (two Heinkel He 111s and one Dornier Do 17) carried out the second attack east to west and destroyed the water supply system, so that after the dropping of the incendiary bombs there was no water in Gernika to put out the fire. As von Richthofen explained: "In the following attacks, 250-kilo bombs were used that destroyed the water pipes, which prevented the work of extinction."[2]
   b. Around 4:35. Three or six Savoia-Marchetti SM.79 bombers attacked the city center. After these first attacks, most of the people assumed, logically, that the bombing was over. The firefighting and relief services went to the center to take care of the wounded and to extinguish the fires. There they would be caught by the next phase of heavy bombing.
2. Around 5:00. Heinkel He 51, Messerschmitt Bf.109, and Fiat

Cr.32 (and perhaps Breguet Br.19s, Heinkel He 45s, Heinkel He 70s reconnaissance aircraft) generated a ring of fire around the town, preventing people from leaving Gernika by machine-gunning anyone trying to flee from the city center. These planes also dropped bombs, since the Heinkel He 51s had six 10-kilo bombs. The Heinkel He 51 had two 7.97 mm MG17 machine guns, each of them firing 20 rounds per second. The Fiat Cr.32 could carry up to 100 kilos of bombs and had two 7.7 mm Breda-SAFAT machine guns firing 13 bullets per second each.

3. Around 5:30. Coming from the north, from the sea, and therefore without their arrival being announced by the alarm systems, the three squadrons K/88 of Junkers Ju 52s bombed Gernika in seven clusters of three aircraft each that executed two or more passes through an aerial corridor of about 150 meters wide (carpet bombing). They launched 250- and 50-kilo explosive bombs with delayed fuses and thousands of incendiary bombs on the city center, flying at an altitude of between 600 and 800 meters. After this attack, the whole of Gernika was in flames.

4. Around 6:15 until 7:40. the fighters and the ground-attack aircraft once again generated a circle of fire around Gernika for about 100 minutes, machine-gunning and bombing survivors of the first phase, who by this time were trying to leave the town by all means.

The 250-kilo bombs had a delayed fuse so that when hitting the target at a speed of about 450 km/h, they perforated buildings of up to five floors, exploding in the base and demolishing the whole building. As a result, shelters in basements were buried under tons of rubble. This was the case for the shelter of Andra Mari and the one in the city hall, among others.

The Andra Mari shelter (approximately 146 m²) was located on the narrow street of that name and consisted simply of a wooden roof and sacks of earth resting on the walls of the buildings on both sides of the street. It suffered the direct impact of two bombs of 250 kilos each that exploded at ground level, causing the façades of the buildings on which this refuge was sustained to collapse on top of the survivors. Those who survived the impact of the 250-kilo bombs and the 50-kilo bombs that followed received during the third phase of the bombardment a shower of incendiary bombs that raised the temperature above 1,500° C, which absorbed the little oxygen available under the debris. As Joxe Iturria, María Madinabeitia, and mayor of Gernika Jose Labauria testified, almost all the people who sought refuge there, between 450 and 500 people in total, died.[3]

But many among them did not die instantly. As expressed by Kaxtor Amunarriz, Francisca Arriaga, José Ramón Urtiaga, and Carmen Zabaljauregi, the cries for help of the people buried under the rubble could still be heard the next day. They were never rescued.[4] Federico Iraeta testified that after the bombing he "started looking around all of the refuges where people had been heard and were known to be still alive. I went to the Santa Maria Refuge and started looking at the debris. Then I saw something moving. It was human legs. They looked like the legs of a girl. The rest of the body was trapped under huge piles of stone and brick. It was impossible to do anything. When I realized all this, I turned and started running. I was through searching. I couldn't bear it any longer."[5]

As Richthofen said laconically, referring to the shelters in Gernika, "the morale effect of the attacks with 100- and 250-kilogram projectiles is very high. There are no possibilities of protection in the shelters unless they are especially [of] resistant construction."[6]

But the informants of the Herrán commission had another point of view. Jesús Obieta, the only witness who reported on what happened in the refuges of Gernika to Herrán, said "that in a certain unnamed shelter were found forty-five dead persons, of whom the corpses had not all been identified, but that they appeared to be those of villagers who had attended the market which had taken place that day in Guernica."[7] This witness confirmed that 45 lifeless bodies were found in a shelter without a name, but the authors of the Herrán Report, based on this and only on this testimony, illegitimately concluded that "in this [Andra Mari] shelter there perished forty-five persons, unhappy inhabitants of the locality who little foresaw their fate."[8] I say illegitimately because it is obvious that Obieta never said that 45 people were killed in the shelter of Andra Mari, since that refuge "had" a name. He meant another refuge, one without a name. On the other hand, Obieta did not say that 45 people died in the said shelter, but that 45 bodies were found there, which, considering that the work of removing the debris in Gernika did not begin until 1939 and did not end until December 1941, is something very different.[9]

But, above all, if Obieta's statements included in the Herrán Report refer to the shelter of Andra Mari, then they are completely inconsistent with the conclusions of the report itself, which included a memorandum on the corpses found in various shelters in the village. According to this memorandum, the recovery of 38 bodies was recorded between May 4 and 29, 1937, 18 of which were identified and 20 of which were not identified. According to the report, 23 of the corpses were found in the shelter of Andra Mari (60.5 percent of the total).[10] In sum, according to the report, 23 bodies were found in Andra Mari and 45 in "a refuge without a name."[11]

Following the logic of the report, the drafters indicated that the victims of Andra Mari had been dynamited by the Reds when they were inside the shelter: "Among other reports, the Commission was informed that various persons knew of the existence of dynamite at that spot, and it was even stated that a carabineer who had knowledge of the fact lost his daughter there because he could not warn her in time, and that he went mad as a result."[12] And, in order to add credibility to the story, the editors tried to explain the way the bombs exploded. According to them, it was very unlikely that a bomb would hit a street as narrow as Andra Mari, which was about 2.67 meters wide. This is true if a single bomb is launched, but if between 31 and 46 tons of explosive are dropped over the city center, it is very likely that one or two of these bombs could impact somewhere in that place. And as Richthofen stated, "250-kilo-gram German breaker projectiles were used in the individual and successive launching mode (*Reihenwurf*) [. . .] When these projectiles [of 250 kilos] hit on a building, the objective completely collapsed."[13]

The Herrán Report also asserted that a bomb explodes against the first thing that impacts, so it would had been impossible for the two 250-kilo bombs to explode at ground level, inside or above the shelter of Andra Mari. But this is also false. As already mentioned, Richthofen stated that the bombs had a delayed fuse, so they went down into [crossed] the buildings before exploding: "After crossing the whole house the explosion [of the 250-kilogram bomb] takes place at ground level, producing funnels of about 0.75 meters deep. The house collapses completely, including its outer walls."[14] But this detail was omitted by the authors of the Herrán Report, who wrote: "It is seen, then, that the bomb reaches the ground with a steep trajectory, and therefore, if it should penetrate into the street between the roofs of the houses there is every probability that before hitting the ground it would bring up against some façade and explode, without making any contact with the sacks forming the roof of the gallery of the shelter. [. . .] Even supposing that this bomb had gone through all the accumulation of obstacles previously described, it is impossible to conceive how it could have penetrated to the sewer, and how the detonator could have survived until that moment to explode, without having previously reacted to the innumerable blows received *en route*."[15]

To conclude, the Herrán Report asserted that a large hole was formed in the surface of Andra Mari Street, "which had none of the characteristics of a crater such as is produced by aerial bombs"[16] and concluded that it was due to the detonation of cartridges of dynamite placed in the public sewage system. The report offered as evidence reference to a "photograph which appears in the lower part of page 18 of the Basque Government brochure, *Guernica*, [in which] a mouth-shaped hole is depicted, within which a great cavity appears. This cavity, which coincides with the street sewer, suggests that a strong explosion occurred therein, which, as has been set out before, could not have been the result of an aerial bomb."[17] However, this is also false, because page 18 of that booklet has no illustration or photograph.

Castor Uriarte, municipal architect of Gernika, told William Smallwood in 1972 that the victims of the Andra Mari shelter could be estimated at around 200, and the victims in other areas of the town between 50 and 100, that is, between 250 and 300 in total. But in 1976 he altered his testimony and estimated the number of fatalities in the shelter of Andra Mari to be 45, conforming in this estimate to the Herrán Report.[18] Vicente Talón expressed some doubts regarding the explanations of the authors of the Herrán Report about the shelter of Andra Mari, but offered the figure of 45 dead without reservations.[19] Jesús Salas went much further.

Given that Andra Mari was one of the "unfinished" shelters of Gernika, Salas, in the three editions of his book, translated the English original from page 24 of the Herrán Report, which states that "in a certain unnamed shelter were found forty-five dead persons,"[20] as "in an unfinished shelter there were 45 dead."[21] Salas was perfectly aware that by translating "without name" with "unfinished" would induce the reader to think of Andra Mari, since that shelter has always been referred to as the "unfinished shelter." And, without mentioning the internal inconsistencies of the report, and accepting its content as a coherent and reliable historical source, under the heading of "The facts and the truth", Salas concluded by asserting that "most of those buried in the shelter of Santa María [Andra Mari], 25, were rescued as of May 4, 1937, and they are recorded in an annex to the Herrán Report."[22] To cover up this improper use and the internal inconsistencies of the source, the author cited in his work the "draft" of the report instead of the report itself as it was published in 1938, which is in the public domain and easily accessible. However, Salas did not mention this, and when he reproduced the report with his translation he wrote: "Annex No. 2. Extract of the testimonies of the witnesses of the Herrán Report."[23] I have not found the alleged draft at any of the fifty archives that I have had access to.

It is inappropriate to leave aside the testimonies of people like Kaxtor Amunarriz, Francisca Arriaga, Federico Iraeta, Joxe Iturria, the mayor of Gernika Jose Labauria, Maria Madinabeitia, Sebastian Uria, José Ramón Urtiaga, and Carmen Zabaljauregi, among others, all of whom were in the refuge or trying to help with the recovery of the corpses, without any data that discredits them. But, from the point of view of the historiographical methodology, it is even more inappropriate to grant credibility to the testimony of Jesús Obieta and the Herrán Report, because, beyond the patent inconsistencies cited here and some even more serious ones that I have indicated throughout this book, by virtue of its origin, nature, content, scientific method, and process of elaboration, this account does not match the facts, lacks credibility and, consequently, cannot be considered a historical source.

Regardless of the nature, lack of coherence, and doubtful credibility of the Herrán Report, affirming that 45 refugees lost their lives in this refuge is totally irrational, as it would mean that the vast majority of people survived two bombs of 250 kilos and many others of 50 kilos in a shelter with only a roof made of wooden beams and sandbags for protection. It would also mean that they also survived the subsequent collapse of the roof and part of the façades of the surrounding buildings, which fell on them. And finally, it would indicate that, after being buried, they survived the fire that devoured the ruins and, fundamentally, that they managed to get out from under the ruins alive even though the rubble was removed months or longer after April 26.

But, despite everything, transgressing the most basic norms of historical research, adulterating translations, and making undue use of illegitimate sources, some will continue to assert that in the Andra Mari shelter 45 people lost their lives and thus erasing the memory of some 450 to 500 people who suffered a horrible death there.

Chapter 22

One hundred and twenty-six people died in the bombing

Reporter Noel Monks was the first to arrive in Gernika and wrote what he saw: "In the good 'I' tradition of the day, I was the first correspondent to reach Guernica, and was immediately pressed into service by some Basque soldiers collecting charred bodies that the flames had passed over. Some of the soldiers were sobbing like children. There were flames and smoke and grit, and the smell of burning human flesh was nauseating. Houses were collapsing into the inferno. In the Plaza, surrounded almost by a wall of fire, were about a hundred refugees. They were wailing and weeping and rocking to and fro."[1] Next to Monks were the reporters Mathieu Corman, Christopher Home, George Steer, and Scott Watson. All of them returned to Bilbao, and some wrote their first articles about the bombing that same night.

The next day, while they were having breakfast, they listened to Radio Sevilla, from which General Gonzalo Queipo de Llano broadcast his program, to hear what the rebel side's version of the events would be. To their surprise, Berlin denied that Gernika had been bombarded on the pretext that the planes had not flown the previous day because of bad weather. That was unexpected, especially considering that at least three of the reporters had been machine-gunned the day before by Heinkel He 51s acting in the outskirts of Gernika, as Steer related: "Then they circled and spotted us. For between fifteen and twenty minutes they dived over our hole at full throttle, loosing off their double guns at us from anything down to two hundred feet. The only thing was to pretend to be dead already, and sometimes we wondered whether we were. Old [Mathieu] Corman was spinning a long story about the ineffectiveness of aerial machine-gunning on entrenched positions, but somehow today he sounded much less impressive, and I asked him to be silent and to wait and see. It struck me, too, as very undignified for an Englishman to eat earth before the German aviation."[2]

After this attack, Corman recalled that they sought refuge in the church of Arbatzegi until the last planes left: "This satanic game with our nerves – with our lives – lasted for about twenty minutes. And the planes, one by one, moved away. We run to the church. We found some survivors of the town grouped in the bell tower. There were eight . . . They cried in silence. They did not dare to leave, lest they saw the broken or burned body of a loved one."[3] The attacks of the morning of April 26 resulted in a considerable number of victims. During the bombing of Arbatzegi (Munitibar), thirty people died and another twelve were wounded, four of which Steer saw as he passed through this town. Canon Alberto Onaindia also saw the corpses and asked a battalion of Basque soldiers to transport them to Bilbao.[4] That same day the planes caused seven deaths and twelve wounded in Markina, and another person lost his life in Arratzu.[5]

In sum, the news from Radio Sevilla shocked the reporters but did not convince them. And, as Monks wrote in his memoirs:

> Then came the last straw, for me. We were sitting round a radio at the Presidencia listening to General de Llano make one of his vile broadcasts to the women of Madrid, telling them, in detail, what to expect from the Moors. Suddenly he switched to Guernica. 'That Señor Monks,' he croaked. 'Don't believe what he writes of Guernica. All the time he was with Franco's forces he was drunk.'"[6] What was nothing more than a tragic joke turned into a serious offense when Monks received a call from the *Daily Express* in London asking him to return to Gernika and verify what he had seen and written the previous day: "'Quiepo de Llano (Franco's foul-mouthed broadcasting general in Seville) says Reds dynamited Guernica during retreat. Please check up!' That felt like a bomb: They were trying to discredit us as liars."[7]

So they returned to Gernika and wrote their chronicles. Monks explained what he saw:

> I went back to Bilbao and wrote my story. I was back at Guernica at daybreak. I saw 600 bodies. Nurses, children, farmers, old women, girls, old men, babies. All dead, torn, and mutilated. Basque soldiers were getting the bodies from the wreckage, many of them weeping. I came to what

had been an air raid shelter. In it were the remains of fifty women and children. A bomb had dropped right through the house into the cellar. Does Franco expect the world to believe that fifty women and children fled into an air raid shelter when their house was mined? Or trapped themselves below there while the house above them was set alight? I went back to Bilbao and wrote another story, just what I had seen. Just as I would have written it if it had been a Franco town in ruins.[8]

Monks did not only write his article, but also asked that it be published with a reproduction of the telegram in which Franco denied that the town had been bombed together with Monks' handwritten signature to be printed so people knew that he was speaking the truth. Days later, Monks would say that "Fact is, I'm a teetotaller. Have been all my life. Ask anyone who knows me. But don't ask me who bombed Guernica. I might take to drink."[9]

Watson, correspondent for the *Star*, also reported counting hundreds of bodies on the spot.[10] And so did canon Alberto Onaindia when he stated that the first hours of the night presented a terrible spectacle of men and women in the woods outside the town searching for their families and friends while "most of the corpses were riddled with bullets."[11] Monks saw 600 bodies for identification, and all the reporters who went to Gernika on the same day, April 26, or in the next two days, estimated the number of deaths above 1,000, except Steer, who put it at about 800.

Today we have 39 accounts from adults who were in Gernika and who testified independently at the time and place where the events occurred, that the deaths were over 1,000.[12] Days later, having established the death toll of those who lost their lives during the bombing and those who died in subsequent days because of injuries received, the Basque government recorded the deaths of 1,654 people. The Basque authorities added that the number of dead was higher, given that they had not been able to clear all the rubble and, as in the case of Andra Mari shelter, the corpses had not been recovered. None of the eyewitnesses registered a number fewer than 800. And this is all the data we have. If we add to the record of 1,654 the 450 or 500 people dead in Andra Mari, the death toll is more than 2,000.[13]

Apart from the aforementioned direct testimonies, we have more than sixty additional adults who were in Gernika performing relief work or helping to recover the corpses, who also gave their testimonies voluntarily and verifiably after the events, many of them in 1972, all of which indicate a number of fatalities over one thousand. In sum, apart from the Basque government's report, we have about a hundred testimonies that provide similar figures, among them nurses from the Karmele Deuna hospital in Gernika, a doctor, a gravedigger and other people directly related to the events, as well as the register of the corpses. And this corpus constitutes 100 percent of the evidence we have, that is, it is coherent and consistent. Finally, note that Gernika had 5,630 inhabitants in 1936 and 3,381 in 1940, four years after the bombing. This means a reduction of 2,249 neighbors, 40 percent of the population.[14]

Obviously, the efforts of the reductionist literature focused on minimizing the number of deaths. This is probably one of the most worrying and ravaging lies about the bombing because, beyond historiographical methodology, trying to erase the memory of the dead is ethically reprehensible.

Joachim von Ribbentrop and Dino Grandi were among the first to reduce the impact of the bombing at the Non-intervention Committee.[15] Also, according to the second conclusion of the Herrán Report, "the number of victims in Guernica on the 26th April did not reach one hundred."[16] This account is based on the testimony of a single informant, Rodolfo Basáñez, who estimated "that the deaths which occurred in Guernica due to the destruction of that town did not amount to one hundred, a point on which he is able to give evidence, because he helped to extract from the ruins of the shelter in Santa Marla Street and of the Calzada Asylum the bodies of those who perished therein."[17]

The editors of the report included a memorandum to the Public Works Commission of the Technical Department of the Francoist government about the corpses found in the various refuges of Gernika. They alleged that some of the names of the victims were registered in the civil registry, although others were missing among those who lost their lives in the course of the attack on the hospital; according to their calculations, this number appeared to be "some twenty-eight," although only nine were registered."[18] The report recorded the recovery of 38 corpses in Gernika between May 4 and 29, 1937: 18 identified and 20 unidentified. Of these 38 bodies, they claimed that 23 were found in the Andra Mari shelter (60.5 percent), although it is documented that Felipe Bastarrechea did not die there, so his body could not have been found in that place.[19]

But we know and have physical evidence that the Francoist authorities did everything in their power to erase the evidence of these deaths, from ripping out books of records to crossing out the names of the dead from the parochial books of the deceased. Corpses also disappeared. As Pedro Agirre testified:

> After troops came into Guernica, men from the surrounding villages were forced to go there and clear away the ruins. I was one of those men. We worked first on the main roads. Then we started working on the side streets. On several occasions we refused to work. There were partly decomposed bodies, and pieces of bodies in that rubble. The nausea, and the thoughts that these had been our friends, made it impossible to work. But each time we stopped, we were threatened and we had to go back. The work was unbearable. We placed handkerchiefs over our noses and mouths and we closed our eyes when we picked up the bodies or pieces of bodies and placed them in our oxen-pulled carts. And we worked until all the streets were clean.[20]

None of these bodies was ever recorded. In fact, between May 29, 1937, and December 1941, when the works for removing all debris in Gernika were finished, after having removed 60,388 m³ of rubble, no corpse was ever registered.[21]

The editors of the Herrán Report were forced to respond to the articles of Monks, Steer, Corman, Holme, and Watson given that, by virtue of their credibility, their writings circulated all around the world. In an ironic tone, the Commission members wrote:

> This political propaganda is couched in a vein of truly apocalyptic extravagance and speaks of thousands of innocent victims cruelly machine-gunned without warning. According to these reports, on that Monday Guernica lay wrapped in its own peaceful existence, far removed from even the whisper of warlike thoughts. It was celebrating its weekly cattle market with all the joy and merriment of a pagan festival. The churches were filled with the usual throngs of worshippers lifting their prayers to the Almighty and assisting at the religious ceremonies. In the orchards and nearby fields every bucolic scene was in full swing. And, so it is alleged, upon this Arcadian idyll there were suddenly launched all the horrors of a ruthless warfare. In the grip of a savage hatred and inspired by a refinement of cruelty our soldiers, so we are

given to understand, mowed down women and children, burned and destroyed their simple homes, and in a few hours converted into a heap of smoking ruins a country town which so short a time before had been the abode of life and innocent happiness.[22]

This idea and tone was repeated by Talón who stated that "the Basque-republican propaganda has reiterated, over the years, the image of Guernica on the eve of the bombing, presenting it as a happy population, without frights, for which war was a distant, unexpected reality to them. This naturally led to the idea that the aircraft surprised the people in Guernica daydreaming, and bombs found them speechless, perishing by the hundreds."[23]

Ricardo de la Cierva was one of the first historians to try to reduce the number of fatalities. In an article published in 1970 in the magazine *Arriba*, he wrote that Gernika was a myth and that "not even a dozen died."[24] Talón and Salas relied solely on the figures of the Herrán Report and accepted them. Corum followed this line: "Picasso all worked to portray Guernica as a massacre of innocent civilians. The official casualty figures of the bombing raid were given as 1,647 dead. This incredibly high figure and the description of the raid as essentially a terror attack have been endlessly repeated since 1937. In reality, the total death toll at Guernica was approximately 300."[25]

None of these authors has ever revealed any document justifying their calculations, apart from the aforementioned Herrán Report, which is based on the testimony of Basáñez. Moreover, few of these authors have cited the 39 testimonies to which I have referred above. And, finally, none of these authors has devoted more than four pages to this aspect of the bombing, limiting themselves simply and plainly to asserting that the figure given by the Basque government is an "exaggeration," without the slightest documentary contribution. More specifically, Corum devoted five lines on page 21 of his work to the calculation of the deaths, and another three lines on page 137, in which the author states that 1,654 dead is an incredibly high number. And, referring to the alleged exaggeration of the Basque government, he quoted himself in footnote no. 22 on page 21. He does not include a single word of the testimonies or other documentary evidence.

Talón described as "completely disproportionate" the figure of 1,654 dead in a line on page 33 of his book and went on to devote the remaining four pages to reinforce the thesis of the Herrán Report, concluding that "the victims of the bombing, as far as I can see, are registered one by one with surprising conscientiousness. So much so that embedded in the list of fallen Franco's battles that followed the capture of Guernica, annotations like this may be read: A militiaman found in the refuge of Santa Maria. That is to say, nobody thought it interesting to hide these supposedly uncomfortable corpses that were emerging as the martyred town was being cleared up of rubble."[26] Talón refers to the copy of the entries included in the memorandum of the Herrán Report, but on the contrary, Humberto Unzueta pointed out in 1997 that the pages of the registry of the Gernika court from April 26 to May 22 were ripped out and the names of the deceased registered in some of the parish books of the locations around Gernika were crossed out. In the case of the civil registry's book of deaths of the city council of Muxika, more than ten of the names were erased, and other names were written on top of them.[27] Likewise, pages 779 to 798 of book No. 71 of the Civil Hospital of Basurto, which included some of the deaths that occurred between January and May 1937, were ripped out.[28]

Salas dedicated five pages of his book to the study of the death toll.[29] He did not comment on the Basque government's registry nor on any of the 39 testimonies, and based his calculation entirely on the Herrán Report, stating that the registry of 1,654 dead "lacks all basis," but without providing any documentation to back his assertion.

Corum even wrote that "[i]n the British Parliament, speeches were made denouncing the attack and inaccurately describing Guernica as an 'open city' that contained no military targets. The Basque government's account of 1,654 dead and 889 wounded was accepted uncritically in the world press although the actual number of dead and wounded was less than a fifth of that number."[30] The author demanded that members of the British Parliament adopt a critical stance, but he offered the reader no explanation as to why 1,654 dead is an "exaggeration."

The calculation of the death toll of the bombing is a matter of historiographical methodology. We have to take all the documents and evidence that we have and study them. But, above all, we must be aware that if we conclude that the dead numbered fewer than 2,000, 1,654, or even 1,000, then the consequences are obvious: Richthofen and Ribbentrop were right that it was a negligible bombardment and, therefore, the document of the Basque government is false and each and every one of the 39 direct witnesses (who were in Gernika, who were adults, who testified freely, who were professionals, etc.) lied in the most shameless way. In short, if the dead were fewer than 1,654, we should grant Queipo de Llano that Monks and Steer and all the other 39 witnesses were liars (or maybe drunk), and we should have that drink with the Australian reporter because there is no reason to doubt Monks when he wrote and signed in his own hand that he "saw" 600 corpses on April 26. And this is so for the simple reason that today there is no documentation or evidence to suggest or allow to prove otherwise. This is how history should be written.

Chapter 23

Witnesses lie and exaggerate

Given that the material evidence, the documentation, and the graphic evidence, as well as the photographs of the material devastation caused by the bombing, are contrary to the Franco regime's alternative versions of the truth, the Herrán Commission was created to provide technical legitimacy to an implausible interpretation of the facts. For this reason, given that the hundreds of oral testimonies that have been compiled offer an explanation of what happened very different from the official truth, delegitimizing the eyewitnesses of the bombing has been a constant in reductionist literature since 1937.

The authors of the Herrán Report spared no effort in emphasizing that the witnesses interviewed by international reporters or the Basque government did not see anything because they were frightened or were in shock, or were in the shelters, concluding that the aforementioned testimonies lack coherence and are, therefore, disposable:

> An aeroplane appeared in the distance flying from the northeast, that is from the sea-coast; some witnesses say at half-past three in the afternoon and others at four. The witnesses do not give any details as to whether the aeroplane was a monoplane or biplane, or whether it had one, two or three motors; the account of each witness varies as to the colour, and none can give any information about its undercarriage, rudders, etc. If there are contradictions and incongruities in respect of its shape and characteristics, the confusion is greater when an attempt is made to throw some light on what it did. Some say that it was alone, others that it was not; some that it machine-gunned from the ground, others that it did the machine-gunning from the air; there are witnesses who declare that it dropped some bombs round about the district of Renteria (see the map), others deny it. In short, the appearance of the aeroplane or aeroplanes can be taken as a fact, but nothing more can be learnt about them, nor about what occurred afterwards in relation

to them. There also appears to be no doubt that the people, frightened by the presence of the aeroplane and by the noise of its engine or engines, hurried to the shelters. Up to a certain point, this explains the confusion of the evidence, since from inside a shelter nothing can be seen of what happens outside and what is heard is confusing. In view of the difficulty of definite evidence from witnesses who were concealed in shelters and not in a position actually to see what occurred above ground during those hours, the Commission decided on a personal inspection.[1]

Martha Howell and Walter Prevenier point out that, in the historiographical and legal sphere, testimony is the solemn attestation of the truth of a fact and a form of evidence obtained from a witness who makes a statement.[2] With regard to oral testimonies, a greater number of independent sources that contain the same or similar message raises the credibility of this message and, consequently, the greater the consistency of the sources, the greater their credibility. Likewise, oral testimonies whose information can be compared with other testimonies and, therefore, are confirmed, turn out to be more reliable than those whose information cannot be compared. Likewise, testimonies produced by expert witnesses (such as war veterans) are considered to be of great value. If two independently generated authoritative testimonies coincide on one issue, the credibility of each of the two sources is significantly higher. Finally, when describing an historical event, primary sources generated by the eyewitnesses of a fact are, naturally, of more value than those generated by third parties.[3]

Gilbert J. Garraghan has explained that oral testimonies are especially relevant when the observer himself or herself reports a fact, when the physical location of the observer allows that person to have direct and certain knowledge of what is reported, when the individual has the physical capacity required to observe what is testified and, finally, when the testimony is not a product of intimidation. This last fact, for example, delegitimizes the Herrán Report's informants. The value of oral testimony is especially prominent when it occurs close to the time at which the events in question took place, as is the case of the 39 testimonies collected in relation to the death toll in Gernika.[4]

All these premises and methodological principles are met in the case of the 60 testimonies referred to in the previous chapter. In conclusion we can say that, by virtue of the quantity, clarity, consistency, coherence, and authority of the testimonies recorded in the case of Gernika, it is methodologically impossible to affirm that "the witnesses did not see what they say they saw" or give as "discredited," "exaggerated," or "irrelevant" the data provided by those without the proper input of material evidence. For this reason, testimonies included in the Machimbarrena or Herrán Reports that due to their origin and nature lack credibility are inadmissible.

Chapter 24

We are not monsters . . .

One of the keys to lying in relation to the execution of this type of atrocity is to state that nobody would be able to do something like that, that human beings would not have been able to carry out an action like the bombing of Gernika. Unfortunately, it is precisely because they were human beings that they behaved as such, because the human animal has that capacity for evil.

The 1937 Luftwaffe's Scientific Section report proposed that "German aviators always scrupulously respected the civilian population," stating that "it was established that, according to the orders, all the aviators had respected the town."[1] Both Adolf Galland and Jaenecke claimed in relation to the bombing of Gernika that the international press tried to deceive the world by representing the German pilots as "Huns, lovers of destruction."[2]

The British intelligence service had special internment camps for thousands of German and Italian prisoners of war in which the conversations between them were recorded without the prisoners' knowledge. Once transcribed, these protocols were declassified after 50 years, in 1996. The conversations include all kinds of material about the brutality of the war in all fields and sectors. In the case of the Luftwaffe, many of the recorded conversations are of this type:

> Pohl: On the second day of the Polish war I had to drop bombs on a station at Posen. Eight of the 16 bombs fell on the town, among the houses, I did not like that. On the third day I did not care a hoot, and on the fourth day I was enjoying it. It was our before-breakfast amusement to chase single soldiers over the fields with M.G. [machine gun] fire and to leave them lying there with a few bullets in the back.
>
> Meyer: But always against soldiers?
>
> Pohl: People (civilians) too. We attacked the columns in the streets.

> I was in the 'Kette' (flight of three aircraft). The leader bombed the street, the two supporting machines the ditches, because there are always ditches there. The machines rock, one behind the other, and now we swerved to the left with all machine guns firing like mad. You should have seen the horses stampede!
>
> Meyer: Disgusting, that with the horses . . .
>
> Pohl: I was sorry for the horses, but not at all for the people. But I was sorry for the horses up to the last day.[3]

Many those interviewed described as "fun" machine-gunning or bombing civilians or, in more extreme cases, like that of a Luftwaffe lieutenant, they said that "throwing bombs has become a passion with me. One itches for it; it is a lovely feeling. It is as lovely as shooting someone down."[4] Corporal Fischer, pilot of a Messerschmitt 109, said, "I can tell you I've killed a lot of people in England! In Folkestone we had definite orders to drop our bombs among the houses. I was called in our Staffel 'the professional sadist.' I went for everything, a bus on the road, a passenger train at Folkestone. We had orders to drop out bombs right into the towns. I fired at every cyclist."[5] The Lieutenant of the Luftwaffe Hans Hastings, of the squadron of fighters No. 26, said that "we were ordered to fire at everything, except military targets. We killed children and women with prams."[6] Fighter pilot V. Greim remembered that "we once made a low-level attack near Eastbourne. When we got there, we saw a large mansion where they seemed to be having a ball or something; in any case we saw a lot of women in fancy-dress, and an orchestra. There were two of us doing long distance reconnaissance. [. . .] We turned round and flew towards it. The first time we flew past, and then we approached again and machine-gunned them. It was great fun!"[7]

These are not exceptions; the National Archives of the United Kingdom preserve more than 50,000 folios transcribed with this type of information, and the National Archives of the United States, about 100,000 pages. As Noel Monks wrote, "Rome put the official seal on Franco's denial, and to this day only 'bad' Catholics believe that the Germans destroyed Guernica. Though doubtless today, after Rotterdam, Coventry, the gas chambers and Belsen, the world doesn't so readily believe that Germans were incapable of pulling off a job like Guernica."[8]

Chapter 25

We are the real victims …

Numerous officers and diplomats involved in the bombing alluded to the defamatory campaign of the "international press" that, in their opinion, had turned a legitimate act of war into a crime in the eyes of humanity. Jaenecke said that the Reds had made a great deal of propaganda with the bombing, obtaining considerable benefits. This rhetoric was used for the first time by Joachim von Ribbentrop at the Non-intervention Committee in May 1937: "We must prevent isolated events from being reported with propagandistic aims."[1] On May 7, 1937, when a proposal for an investigation into the bombing was presented to the Non-intervention Committee, Franco's General Headquarters sent a telegram to General Sperrle refusing to carry out such an investigation, which he called a "propaganda maneuver and disrepute of National Spain and friendly nations."[2]

Likewise, Rear Admiral Bohem, commander of the observation forces of the Condor Legion, opined that the bombing of Gernika "has been exaggerated by England for politico-tactical reasons, since it is evident that a pretext was sought that, in the cloak of humanity, hide commercial interests in the lands of northern Spain."[3] The authors of the Luftwaffe's War Scientific Section stated that the bombing had been used "by the entire hostile world press" to blame German air units for the destruction of the town in order to produce the most violent state of mind against the Germans.[4]

Lieutenant Hans von Beust, head of the second Junkers Ju 52 squadron that bombed Gernika, asserted that the attack was discussed all over world for propagandistic reasons.[5] According to Beust, the smoke produced by the bombing of the first Junkers Ju 52 squadron was of such magnitude that they no longer saw the target and launched their bombs blindly, destroying "unthinkingly" the city center of Gernika, and "this failure, purely technical in itself, was used astutely as propaganda by the other side in such a way that Franco had to fear political inconveniences, and the whole attack was simply denied as a result."[6]

The Herrán Report included this same line of thought, stating that the destruction of Gernika "was carefully premeditated"["an attempt has been made to utilise its destruction for purposes of political propaganda, blending it with other events of what happened at the same time in other places, and confounding the whole issue with clever and insidious distortion of the facts."[7] This is the idea encapsulated in conclusions 13 and 14 of that report: "(XIII) Apart from the complex political factors involved and its use as worldwide propaganda, the burning of Guernica is similar in its cause and effect to that of Irun, Eibar and Potes. (XIV) The campaign of political propaganda of which Guernica has been made the subject has no basis in fact, but is a clever blend of unrelated happenings which in no way approximate to reality."[8]

Many years later, the idea was taken up again by Adolf Galland, Condor Legion Heinkel He 51 pilot, one of the people who went to Gernika to study the ruins of the town. In the Spanish version of his book published in 1955, he wrote that the issue of Gernika was "a reason for dejection in the ranks of the Legion" and that the pilots "did not like to talk about Guernica." But this is not true, for as Lieutenant Beust wrote, the pilots of the Condor Legion were forbidden to speak of the bombing and were even ordered to deny that it had happened. However, Galland believed that "the opposing side talked a 'Blue streak' about it and the Reds extracted from that unfortunate event considerable propagandistic benefit. It was not really an open city, nor was it destroyed. It was simply one of the innumerable errors that, later, during the World War II, both sides also committed. Even today, after Rotterdam, Warsaw, Hamburg, Kessel, Rothenburg, and Berlin, even after the horrors of Dresden, Guernica continues to act as a phantom ghost of anti-German resentment."[9]

And, as in all other cases, these versions have infiltrated the historiographical literature on Gernika. Müller said in 2008 that this episode, "world famous thanks to Picasso's painting, was used by British propaganda to support the thesis that it was Göring's Luftwaffe that initiated the strategic air war."[10] Salas referred in his book to the "waves of international propaganda," and Talón, under the heading of "more ink than bombs," asserted that "it has been said that more tons of ink than bombs fell on Guernica. And it is a great truth. As also it is that most of that ink ran on the paper kneaded in coven images and Goyaesque nightmares, very often exaggerated or purely and simply, imagined. In my collection of documents, I keep a whole series of spooky stories. There are those who wrote of streets turned into mats of milled human flesh, of heaps of unrecognizable dead, of children disheveled with their guts fried in the heat of fire and even of a girl whom the explosion of a bomb projected against a wall, being converted in a bas-relief sculpted in viscera and blood."[11]

It is disturbing that someone believes that the bombing of a town can be described without reference to Goyaesque images and unrecognizable corpses, or even bodies that would never be recovered. The girl crushed against a wall to which Talón refers as a myth was one of the two daughters of María Olabarria. This is her mother's account:

> From the place where we were, we saw the bombs fall. The planes circled and circled above us. It seemed that they were looking for us. And it was true: they were looking for four women. There was a farmhouse nearby. We ran towards the entrance. It was closed. Then we stuck materially to the door frame trying to protect each other. I was in the middle. An airplane circled the farmhouse, firing with the machine gun. Earth jumped in front of us. Suddenly we heard a frightful crunch: a bomb had fallen on the farmhouse. The explosion threw me to the ground among stones and bricks. My oldest daughter, who was twenty-seven, died instantly, crushed. The other, the youngest, who was going to get married, had time to hold my hand, squeeze it a little and exclaim: 'Ay!' She sighed, and with her eyes fixed on me, she died. I do not know how long I was there between my two dead daughters. The blood ran down my neck. After a while they picked me up.[12]

It seems that Talón was unaware of the effect of temperatures above 1,500° C on the human body but, in fact, some people died burned, destroyed by the explosions and with their bellies outside their bodies, because that is the effect that the explosive and incendiary bombs produce in a human organism. Such was the case of one of the Garzes sisters. And so, Juan Sistiaga, crying, told an interviewer thirty-five years after the events:

> There was a big mansion just north of a small plaza in the northeast section of Guernica. The mansion had a stone wall around it and a bomb had fallen and broken part of the wall. Lying nearby were two girls and

a man who must have taken refuge near the wall. The man and one of the girls were dead. The other girl was still alive, but her abdomen had been torn open and her intestines were hanging out. Her eyes were open and they seemed to be pleading to me for help. I knew that she was mortally wounded but I knelt down and she struggled to get up. I held her under the shoulders and tried to assure her that a stretcher was on the way and that we would take her to the hospital as soon as possible. She just looked at me. She never said anything. She was a very beautiful girl with light brown hair. I was still holding her and talking to her, and waiting for a stretcher, when I heard the sound of airplanes. I looked back over my shoulder and saw them. They were those ugly three-motored German bombers. They were low and right upon us. I turned and looked back at the girl. She was dead. I had seen death many times on the front but a wave of emotion came over me. I laid her down gently and motioned for the other *gudariak* [Basque soldiers] to take cover.[13]

Chapter 26

The bombing of Gernika is a myth

One of the effects of lying is the double negation of the facts. Reduced to its smallest dimension or simply denied, historical reality appears to the eyes of revisionist authors as "myth" or "legend," that is, as fiction. It is remarkable, however, to note that all these authors have written so much about this event, which, in their opinion, did not go beyond the anecdotal. Ricardo de la Cierva explained it this way:

> Guernica is, therefore, two totally different things: a historical fact and a legend entrenched in the world public opinion. The legend has covered in such a way the reality that has become a very accredited myth, and even a topic among specialized authors [. . .]). In the early afternoon of April 26, the city of Guernica had practically disappeared after a terrible aerial bombardment; and an immense wave of propaganda and disinformation emerged those same days and has reached us in the form of a mythological construction that continues to conceal from many people the reality of what happened there.[1]

Some years later, Salas and Talón alluded to the "myth" or "legend" of Gernika in the same terms. Talón, like Salas before him, pointed to reporter George Steer as the author of the myth, which would later be perpetuated by Picasso: "Steer reiterates in the pages of the book [*The Tree of Gernika*] what he had written in *The Times*. He does not detract from anything and exposes, one by one, all the most propagandistic ingredients of the myth, such as, for example, the distance from Guernica to the front, the bucolic aspect of the city that Monday in April, the priests comforting the crowd, etc."[2]

Contrary to Talón's claim, these "ingredients of the myth" are documented. Father Endeiza and two other priests prayed the rosary in the shelter of the city hall; Father Laudate did the same in one of the shelters in the Plaza de la Union. Two Jesuits, the brothers Fidel and Juan Jose Goikoetxea, were for a time in the church of Andra Mari and, later, while the first stayed with those who had sought refuge in that church, the other went out to help the wounded in the streets: "Father Juan Jose advised us to do an act of penance and then he absolved us of our sins and told us that we would all go to heaven if we died then."[3] As Joseba Elosegi related, Father Arronategi was also in the church of Andra Mari, and numerous witnesses claim to have seen him with Father Andres Untzain helping people during the bombing in different parts of Gernika: "In Barrenkale I met with our chaplain, Don Andres [Untzain] who, together with the parish priest of Gernika, Father Arronategi, helped the dying. I found Don Andres desperate and pale as death. He told me, 'Get out of here; they are going to kill us all.'"[4] As Monks reported, "Some [planes] descended low and machine-gunned the streets. Father Arronategi behaved marvelously. He prayed with the people in the plaza, while the bombs were falling."[5] Arronategi himself corroborated the same thing when he stated that "with a heart full of pain, [another priest] quickly administered the last of the most sacred sacraments of the Catholic faith to those who were suffering death rattles. [. . .] To those who listen to me, I say, I have seen all these things with my own eyes."[6]

Canon Alberto Onaindia also assisted the victims:

I had not gone far when a plane approached and forced me to jump into a ditch to protect myself. A woman and a child running in front of me did not make it. A bomb fell between us. It was a loud explosion. I immediately left the ditch and ran towards the woman and the child. Other people also came to help. Someone said that the boy was the godson of the woman. Medically, there was nothing I could do for them. The bomb had not produced marks on their bodies, but I noticed that the blood ran down their chins; his internal organs had been destroyed by the explosion. I gave them absolution and stayed with them until I was certain that they had died.[7]

The Passionist priest Victoriano Gondra, Aita Patxi, also helped the wounded in the hospital during the bombing and was wounded himself.[8]

In 2008 Corum wrote: "The facts about the bombing of Guernica bear little resemblance to the myth"[9] and added that "there was nothing new about the attack on Guernica. Other villages on the Basque front lines, notably the town of Durango in late March, had been bombed in a similar fashion."[10] A according to Corum, the Luftwaffe regularly used about 60 aircraft and launched between 31 and 46 tons of bombs on targets less than one square kilometer in which between 10,000 and 12,000 civilians were crowded. One thing is right though: prior to the bombing of Gernika, the Luftwaffe and, in general, rebel aviation, had executed more than 600 bombing operations on Basque soil.[11]

Corum wrote that "ironically, the attack on Guernica, which made for a brief flurry of proSpanish Republican propaganda, ultimately proved of great advantage to the Third Reich. Because the sensational press coverage gave the impression that Guemica was a city instead of a small town, the Luftwaffe was credited with the ability to wipe whole cities off the map – something far beyond the capability of the German air force at that time. The press had already been conditioned to expect the destruction of whole cities by air and believed that "terror bombing" would be a feature of a future war. In Spain, it appeared that the future had arrived. The exaggerated reports of Guernica had the effect of confirming the predictions of the airpower theorists concerning civilian casualties."[12]

Corum was right. Göring did everything in his power to spread the image of an all-powerful German air force, but as the facts would show, the Luftwaffe was less capable and far less effective than Hitler himself believed, seemed to believe, or wanted to believe. But it is not true that the predictions of air power theorists about civilian casualties would fall short. I do not know what Corum is referring to when he considers the 1937 predictions exaggerated, but it is a fact that eight years later World War II was sealed with two separate terror bombings (the atomic bombings of Hiroshima and Nagasaki) that caused the instant death of more than 200,000 people, most of them civilians.

Chapter 27

The bombing of Gernika was not a crime

Some authors have denied that the bombing of Gernika was a crime. The reasons underlying this debate are technical and legal, not necessarily ethical. According to these authors, bombing from the air was not a crime given the international legislation of the time, so it was not "illegal" to destroy towns and cities. Leaving aside the ramifications of this issue, and the fact that it is difficult to argue that killing civilians from the air is different from killing civilians on land, almost no one denies that the bombing of Gernika was an atrocity. The issue is that, according to some authors, this atrocity was never brought before a court of justice and, therefore, has not been considered a crime in court.

In application of the provisions of articles 237 and 238 of the Military Code, Hans J. Wandel, Heinkel He 51 pilot, was tried and convicted by a court in Bilbao on May 26, 1937, for having participated in the bombing of Gernika and, as such, for being a collaborator of the military coup and, therefore, responsible for conspiracy and rebellion against the Republican government. Notwithstanding this ruling, a competent court has never considered the bombing. Relying on this technicality, but without explaining what it means or documenting it, Corum stated that "Richthofen was not a war criminal for directing the bombing of Guernica, Warsaw, and Stalingrad. These were harsh acts of war – but not crimes under the international law and norms of the era."[1] And Müller concluded that "until now the bombing of Gernika has been considered the beginning of the aerial terror bombings, a legend that the specialized bibliography has refuted for some time."[2]

Considering the lack of a positive norm in relation to terror bombing or the bombing of open cities in 1937, the cases seen by the Popular Court of Bizkaia against German pilots represent some of the few examples of conviction on the basis of the principles of aerial warfare.

Though the Basque government released the three aviators in 1937, Walter Kienzle, Günther Schulze-Blank, and Wandel were captured, taken to prison, tried, sentenced, and convicted by Basque courts of justice, charged with conspiracy, rebellion, and homicide by virtue of their participation in attacks such as the one against Gernika.[3]

Apart from all this, the bombing of Gernika, like all the bombings executed in the Basque Country by the German and Italian air forces, constituted a clear violation of the Non-intervention Pact that the Italian and the German regimes had endorsed at the end of August 1937. From this perspective, the bombing of Gernika is undoubtedly a war crime, since it transgressed the norms that, at an international level, had been agreed on during the war of 1936 prior to the bombing of April 26. And this principle, as already indicated, is applicable to all the bombings on the Spanish mainland coordinated by the Luftwaffe and the Aviazione Legionaria between 1936 and 1939.

But, above all, the fact that taking the life of civilians has not been declared a "crime" by an international court of justice does not mean and should not mean that it does not constitute a serious atrocity and a reprehensible act.

Chapter 28

If it were not for Picasso …

The logical consequence of the 27 lies discussed so far is that the bombing of Gernika does not deserve to be remembered, since it was no more than a collateral event in the context of a war. Ribbentrop first formulated this idea within the Non-intervention Committee when in May 1937 he stated that the Gernika issue should not be debated when all the members of the committee were aware of the "continued Red terror" in the Republican field:

> The Committee should avoid the danger of interfering in an internal Spanish matter. In the later course of the debate, and especially in view of the aggressive comments made by the Swedish delegate about the Guernica incident, without mentioning Germany, I was surprised by the fact that the question of the humanization of the civil war, in spite of the continued Red terror, had suddenly entered the discussions of the Committee now, with clear propagandistic connection to the news from the newspapers about certain incidents of recent times.[1]

Nine years later, Hermann Göring stated at the Nuremberg trials that the Allies had also bombed cities and that, consequently, there was nothing "illegitimate" in these events. But like many others before him, invoking *cæteris paribus* did not help Göring, nor Ribbentrop, and both were found guilty and sentenced to death in Nuremberg for their crimes because the perpetration of atrocities at the hands of others does not mitigate their own guilt.

Returning to the idea that the bombing of Gernika was an irrelevant event, Vicente Talón asserted and wrote in 1987 that if Picasso had not hung his canvas in Paris in 1937, nobody would had ever have known what happened there.[2] Müller also said that the bombing is now "world-famous thanks to Picasso's painting."[3] They were wrong. In fact, Picasso began working on his work on May 1 and finished it on June 4, 1937, but the canvas was not displayed to the public in the pavilion of the Republic for the World Exposition in Paris until July 12. By then Gernika had jumped to the front pages of the European and American press.

A sampling of U.S. newspapers reveals that between April 27 and 30, 1937, an average of 150 daily news stories or a total of 600 news stories about the bombing were published (about 100 on April 27, 120 on April 28, 170 on April 29, and 210 on April 30).[4] Without being exhaustive, my research reveals that the number of news articles about the bombing of Gernika in the North American press before July 12, 1937, exceeds 7,000, and 80 percent of those that appeared on April 27 were published on the front page.[5] The *New York Times* published 63 articles on the bombing in the 76 days that separate April 26 from July 14, and *La Vanguardia de Catalunya* published a total of 93 articles about the bombing in 1937, 72 of them before Picasso hung his canvas in Paris.

In short, contrary to what Talón and Müller claimed, practically everyone who read a newspaper on either of the two continents knew about the bombing of Gernika long before they knew that Picasso had begun to paint his masterpiece. Picasso decided to dedicate his canvas to Gernika because he knew that this would provoke a reaction in a public already familiar with the chronicle of the bombing.

About a month before Picasso's *Guernica* was shown for the first time, the editor of the pamphlet *Foreign Wings over the Basque Country* wrote that

> the episode of Guernica, with all that it represents both in the military and the moral order, seems destined to pass into History as a symbol. A symbol of many things, but chiefly of that capacity for falsehood possessed by the new Machiavellism which threatens destruction to all the ethical hypotheses of civilization. A clear example of the use which can be made of untruth to degrade the minds of those whom one wishes to convince. And so, over against the truth, the legend of what happened in Guernica is being formed. And whatever it lacks in poetry this legend is at least a revelation of dark corners in the human mind.[6]

He was not wrong, because he did not intend to lie.

Chapter 29

Franco Savior, Franco Merciful, Franco Architect of Peace

The transmission of the lie through official channels, the diffusion of the "truth of the dictatorship," generated protocols, a certain liturgy, and solemn ceremonies, with all the pomp and circumstance that the propaganda of the Francoist regime diligently treasured. In the case of Gernika, the ritualization of the lie took the form of hagiography, and this adds two more lies to the long list of falsehoods in the Gernika case: Franco savior and merciful (in relation of Franco's adoption of Gernika), and Franco architect of peace (in reference to the reconstruction of the town).

The regime used the reconstruction of Gernika and the rest of the towns destroyed during the war as a means of propaganda. The Press Office of the Directorate for Devastated Regions published and distributed between 1940 and 1956 the magazine *Reconstruction* with a resounding message: "Let's drown so much evil [the fire of Gernika] with the greatest good that is kindness, truth and justice."[1]

By virtue of the decree of September 23, 1939, of the Ministry of the Interior that Franco himself had signed, Franco was authorized to "adopt" those localities that had suffered extreme damage during the war. "To facilitate and discipline national reconstruction," the said decree regulated the "adoption of cities damaged by war," whereby the Head of State arranged the general plan for reconstruction and, "where appropriate, of sanitation, internal improvement, widening and extension" of the affected cities.[2]

The regime's media turned Franco into "the architect of peace" in public opinion.

Just before the adoption decree was passed, the Provincial Government of Bizkaia entrusted the sculptor José María Garrós in August 1939 with the preparation of three crucifixes carved with wood from the tree of Gernika for the Pope, for Franco, and for the hall of the Bizkaian Provincial Council. Coinciding with the reception of the cross, Franco "granted" to Gernika the benefits of an "adopted town" by virtue of the decree of October 26, 1939, together with Belcaire, Lleida, Orjiva, Porcuna, Villanueva de la Barca, and Zarza-Capilla.

Under Article 3 of the aforementioned decree, Franco would enjoy full powers of expropriation on land, lots and property, and rights of all kinds that "for cases of internal improvement of the towns" were granted to city councils and private companies. He would also have the full right to "verify a new subdivision and distribution of lots in the part of the town subject to the new urbanization plans."[3] In addition, the sixth article prescribed that the compulsory expropriations that the State carried out for the reconstructions might impose the obligation to accept, as compensation for the old lots, others of equivalent value, located in the new subdivision. Moreover, the state reserved the right to compel the recipients of compensations for expropriation to have the amount of said expropriation invested in reconstruction works.

All this meant, in sum, that those families who had lost their homes during the bombing had a period of no more than fifteen days to claim legal ownership of their homes. However, families repressed from the war experience or with members considered "not adept" to the regime did not have the opportunity to claim their properties. With the expropriation materialized, the State invested in the construction of low-cost and low-quality housing that would later rent or sell to its former or new owners. These expropriations and the reparcelling were presented to the public as a necessary renovation and improvement of the urbanism of the town, which until July 18, 1936, had grown "disorderly." According to the architect of the General Directorate for Devastated Regions Gonzalo Cárdenas, "Guernica will once again be remade with that typical and traditional beauty that must be a legitimate pride of the land of Biscay."[4]

In short, Gernika was expropriated and sold in public auction for the benefit of the authorities of the dictatorship, while Franco was shown through the propaganda channels of the regime as a benefactor, adoptive father, and merciful soul of those towns that had suffered the incendiary torch of "the Reds and the Separatists." And the magazine *Reconstruction* published the photos of the new Gernika with these words: "The ashes gave way to a thriving life that has started a new era for the provincial town. And where war and hatred nailed the Inri of destruction, the constructive peace has raised the Spanish response of a 'Here is Guernica,' which disdained the good reasons in order to embrace authentic works, which represent true love."[5]

After this phase of the reconstruction, on February 13, 1946, Franco, "Caudillo de la Reconstrucción," was named adopted son of Gernika. In commemoration of Franco's "thirty years of peace" and, on January 29, 1966, the city council of Gernika granted the dictator the *"medalla de brillantes al mérito de la villa"* medal.

Epilogue

Passion for Ignorance

Salas introduced in his book about the bombing a section entitled "The Myth and the Legend," to which he contrasted another section under the title "The Facts. The Truth," wherein he enumerated "the elements of the legend" of Gernika. De la Cierva liked the idea and recorded the eight "lies" about Gernika in his 2003 book in this way:

According to Jesús Salas the main elements of the Guernica legend are still the following at this point:

1. Guernica was an open village of 7,000 inhabitants without military interest.
2. Because the bombing occurred on Monday, market day, the population reached 10,000, which increased the number of deaths. There was, of course, no military presence in the population.
3. Guernica was not a tactical target and therefore lacked military traffic at that time.
4. The attack was carried out exclusively by the German aviation.
5. The bombing lasted three long hours, and civilians were mown down with machine-gun fire on the streets.
6. The destruction was caused by the combination of explosive and incendiary bombs.
7. The number of victims was very high: 1,654, or more than 3,000 according to others.
8. There was a meeting in Burgos at which the bombing was planned. It was held on April 25, with a range of attendees, according to the views of each promoter of the legend; some even indicate General Franco's participation in the decision.[1]

Except for the fourth and eighth premises, the rest of the presumed elements of the legend are documentable and documented historical facts. And this tradition continues even today, in 2018, because lies are contagious. In reference to George Steer, Jorge Vilches has affirmed, without any documentary evidence to support his point, that "his data were false: there was no market, not ten thousand people, not hundreds of deaths."[2] The constant repetition of the lie reveals that Susan Hilton's observation is true: "I lie to myself all the time, but I never believe me."

In a certain sense, the denial of the bombing of Gernika is the story of the exaltation of lie and an example applicable to the social psychology of the Lacanian concept of passion for ignorance. There is still something in our society that makes us unable to acknowledge and accept historical facts. Freud explained it by affirming that, if the perception of reality produces us sorrow, restlessness, or disgust, we tend to sacrifice the truth. This turns the lie, at last, into an act of cowardice and a serious lack of responsibility.

Talón preferred to explain the history of the denial of the bombing by explaining that there were bigger and more urgent interests, so Franco was forced to lie: "General Franco had to adopt, in the midst of the war, a coordinated attitude with that of propaganda and deny any participation, either of its own or of its allies, in the destruction of the provincial town."[3] This is undoubtedly the theory of the historical (and political) narrative of hyperrealist postmodernism, a dangerous trend of thought based on the principle that in order to preserve the slightest fragment of public legitimacy it is necessary to create an alternative reality.

In reference to Ángel Viñas, Talón wrote frivolously that "the bad thing about these pamphleteers of history is that they often do not read themselves and take from others what is convenient for them, rejecting the rest and, as a consequence, it is a child's play to make them look bad."[4] Apparently, for some historians, writing about this or other topics is child's play, or a ring for insults. Not so. When writing about the bombing of Gernika or any other atrocity, it must be acknowledged that referents are physical persons who suffered a slow, painful, and horrible death, many of them without having had the opportunity to reach adulthood. It is the responsibility of each person to unearth the truth by showing due respect to the victims, regardless of where they died and to set the record straight with regard to the role of the executioner at the hands of whom they perished. This is the responsibility of historians.

Notes

Author's Preface

1 For a documented explanation of these facts see Xabier Irujo, *El Gernika de Richthofen. Un ensayo de bombardeo de terror* (Gernika: Gernikako Bakearen Museoa Fundazioa/Gernika-Lumoko Udala, Gernika, 2012), 151–162.

2 "El prisionero de ayer. Wandel hace la experiencia de los 500 metros," *El Liberal* 37, no. 12598, May 14, 1937, 1, 3.

3 *Foreign Wings over the Basque Country* (London: The Friends of Spain, London, 1937), pp. 17–20.

4 *Foreign Wings over the Basque Country*, p. 18.

5 "El prisionero de ayer. Wandel hace la experiencia de los 500 metros," *El Liberal* 37, no. 12598, May 14, 1937, 1, 3.

6 "German pilot is shot down," *Reno Evening Gazette*, Tuesday, May 13, 1937, 1.

7 Isidro Gomá, *Pastorales de la guerra de España* (Madrid: Ediciones Rialp, 1955), 71.

8 Adam Jones, *Genocide: A Comprehensive Introduction* (New York: Routledge, 2011), 517–525.

9 Klaus A. Maier, *Guernica. La intervención alemana en España y el "caso Guernica"* (Madrid: Sedmay, 1976), 188.

I Italy and Germany did not intervene

1 Letter of Johannes Welczeck to the Minister of the Exterior Konstantin von Neurath. Paris, August 2, 1936. Documents on German Foreign Policy (1918–1945), Series D (1937–1945), Volume III, Germany and the Spanish Civil War (1936–1939), Department of State (Washington D.C.: USGPO, 1950), 22.

2 Paul Preston and Ann L. Mackenzie, eds., *The Republic Besieged: Civil War in Spain 1936–1939* (Edinburgh: Edinburgh University Press, 1996), 41–42. See also Irujo, *El Gernika de Richthofen*, 31–32.

3 Claude Bowers, *My Mission to Spain* (New York: Simon and Schuster, 1954), 325.

4 Report of Alexander Kirk, attaché to the U.S. embassy in Rome, to the Secretary of State. Rome, May 14, 1937. National Archives and Records

Administration [NARA], U.S. Department of State Files 1930–1939 (Files 852.00/ . . . , Box 6400), Document 852.00/5518.

5 *Memoria*. Rome, January 6, 1937. NARA, RG 242. Foreign Records Seized Collection. Papers of Count Ciano (Lisbon Papers) received from the Department of State. Microfilm Publication T816, R. 1, 167–169.

6 This booklet was published in three languages, Spanish, English, and French. The original title was "La agresión italiana. Documentos ocupados a las unidades italianas en la acción de Guadalajara." The Spanish Situation. Report by Ambassador Claude G. Bowers to the U.S. Secretary of State. May 31, 1937. NARA, College Park, U.S. Ambassador Claude G. Bowers Files (Files 852.00/ . . . , Boxes 3687 to 3701), Document 852.00/5676.

7 Note of Ray Atherton, advisor to the U.S. Embassy in London, to the State Department. London, May 5, 1937. NARA, College Park, U.S. Ambassador Claude G. Bowers Files (Files 852.00/ . . . , Boxes 3687 to 3701), Document 852.00/5602, p. 8.

8 Report by Ralph C. Stevenson, consul of the United Kingdom in Bilbao, to the British Ambassador Sir Henry Chilton. Bilbao, April 28, 1937, inn W. N. Medlicott and Douglas Dakin, eds., *Documents on British Foreign Policy (1919–1939)* (London: Her Majesty's Stationery Office, 1980), 696–698.

9 Telegram from Joachim von Ribbentrop, German ambassador in London, to the Ministry of Foreign Affairs in Berlin. London, May 6, 1937, in *Documents on German Foreign Policy (1918–1945), Series D (1937–1945), Volume III, Germany and the Spanish Civil War (1936–1939)*, 283.

10 "Interpelación de Vandervelde sobre la destrucción de Guernica," *La Vanguardia*, Wednesday, May 25, 1937, 6.

11 The minutes of the non-intervention committee and its subcommittees are found in a large number of files, including in the British national archives of Kew or in the archives of the Ministry of Foreign Affairs of Rome.

12 Fernando Díaz-Plaja, *La Guerra Civil, 1936–1939* (Barcelona: Plaza & Janés, Barcelona, 1971), 244.

13 Letter of Richthofen dated May 25, 1937, in Maier, *Guernica. La intervención alemana en España y el "caso Guernica"*, 88.

14 *Proa*, 126, León, April 29, 1937. It was also partially reproduced in the Euzkadi newspaper on April 28.

15 Joachim von Ribbentrop, *The Ribbentrop Memoirs* (London: Weidenfeld and Nicolson, 1953), 70.

2 It was a civil and Spanish war

1 *The Manchester Guardian*, September 28, 1936.

2 Letter of Russel Thayer, secretary of the North American Society to Aid

Spanish Democracy, to Franklin D. Roosevelt. New York, August 30, 1937. NARA, U.S. Department of State Files 1930–1939 (Files 852.00/. .., Box 6404), Document 852.00/6457.

3 Isidro Gomá, *Respuesta obligada del cardenal arzobispo de Toledo Isidro Gomá Tomás* (Iruñea: s.n., 1937).

4 Gomá, *Pastorales de la guerra de España*, 51–53.

5 Gomá, *Pastorales de la guerra de España*, 71.

6 *League of Nations Official Journal* (March–April 1937): 264.

7 A year before, on January 2, 1937, the Italian regime had signed a "gentlemen's agreement" with the British administration, according to which the two governments recognized the others' interests in the Mediterranean.

8 *Lessons from the Spanish War*. The Command and General Staff School. Fort Leavenworth, Kansas, December 14, 1937. NARA, RG 165. Records of the Military Intelligence Division Relating to Conditions in Spain (1918–1941). Microfilm Publication MI.1445, R. 7.

9 *Congressional Record. Appendix of the First Session of the 75th Congress of the U.S.A. Volume 81, Part 9, January 5, 1937 to May 19, 1937* (Washington, D.C.: USGPO, 1937), 1131.

10 Telegram from the Ambassador to the French republic to the Secretary of State, Paris, February 20, 1937, in *Foreign Relations of the United States, Diplomatic Papers, 1937*, 47.

11 Letter from the Ambassador in Spain to the Secretary of State, Jean de Luz, January 12, 1937, in *Foreign Relations of the United States, Diplomatic Papers, 1937*, 255.

12 Bowers, *My Mission to Spain*, 354.

13 Report to the U.S. Secretary of State. May 18, 1937. NARA, College Park, U.S. Ambassador Claude G. Bowers Files (Files 852.00/ . . . , Boxes 3687 to 3701), no reference. Between Documents 852.00/5602 and 852.00/5641.

14 Report by the Ambassador of the Spanish Republic to the United States, Fernando de los Ríos, to the U.S. Secretary of State. June 4, 1937. NARA, College Park, U.S. Ambassador Claude G. Bowers Files (Files 852.00/ . . . , Boxes 3687 to 3701), Document 852.00/5735.

15 *Congressional Record. Appendix of the First Session of the 75th Congress of the U.S.A.* Volume 81, Part 9, January 5, 1937 to May 19, 1937, pp. 1131, USGPO, Washington, 1937.

16 Joint Resolution 390, 75th Congress, 1st Session, House of Representatives, June 1, 1937.

17 Letter of senator Jerry O'Connell to the State Secretary Cordell Hull. Washington D.C., June 2, 1937. NARA, U.S. Ambassador Claude G.

Bowers Files (Files 852.00/ . . . , Boxes 3687 to 3701), Document 852.00/5629.

18 Report 6.895 of coronel Stephen O. Fuqua. Valencia, October 18, 1937. NARA, RG 165. Records of the Military Intelligence Division Relating to Conditions in Spain (1918–1941). Microfilm Publication MI.1445, R. 12.

19 Biddle, Anthony J. D., *Poland and the Coming of the Second World War: The Diplomatic Papers of A. J. Drexel Biddle, Jr., United States Ambassador to Poland, 1937–1939* (Columbus: Ohio State University, 1976), 12.

20 Letter of Russel Thayer, Secretary of the North American Society to Aid Spanish Democracy, to Franklin D. Roosevelt. New York, August 30, 1937. NARA, U.S. Department of State Files 1930–1939 (Files 852.00/ . . . , Box 6404), Document 852.00/6457.

21 Montanari, Bruno, *Appunti sull'impliego dei mezzi aerei per gli allievi del terzo corso regolare della R.A.A.*, Regia Accademia Aeronautica, Caserta, 1942. NARA, RG 242. Foreign Records Seized Collection. Collection of Italian Military Records, 1935–1943. Microfilm Publication T821, R. 461, 85–241, p. 115.

22 *Al comando di truppe volontarie*, June 28, 1937. USSME, F. 18, *Informazioni Ufficio "I" sulla situazione político-militare nazionale e rossa (giugno–ottobre 1937)*.

23 Paul Preston, *Franco: A Biography* (New York: Basic Books/HarperCollins, 1994), 161.

24 Adolf Hitler, *Hitler's Table Talk, 1941–1944: His Private Conversations* (New York: Enigma Books, 1951), 569.

3 No market was held in Gernika

1 *Guernica. Being the Official Report of a Commission Appointed by the National Government to Investigate the Causes of the Destruction of Guernica on April 26–28, 1937* (London: Eyre & Spottiswoode Ltd., London, 1938), 2–3.

2 *Guernica. To civilized mankind* ([Bilbao:] [Gobierno de Euskadi], 1937), 5–6.

3 *Guernica. To civilized mankind*, 5–6.

4 Jean Tarragó (Victor Montserrat), *Le drame d'un peuple incompris. La guerre au Pays Basque* (Paris: H. G. Peyre, 1937), 75.

5 *Guernica. Being the Official Report of a Commission Appointed by the National Government to Investigate the Causes of the Destruction of Guernica on April 26–28, 1937*, Eyre & Spottiswoode ltd., London, 1938, 16.

6 *Guernica. Being the Official Report . . .* , 24–25.

7 *Guernica. Being the Official Report . . .* , 23.

8 *Guernica. Being the Official Report* . . . , 3.

9 Vicente Talón, *El holocausto de Guernica* (Barcelona: Plaza & Janés, 1987), 39–40.

10 Talón, *El holocausto de Guernica*, 39–40.

11 Irujo, *El Gernika de Richthofen*, 95–96.

12 María Jesús Cava Mesa, María Silvestre, and Javier Arranz, *Memoria colectiva del bombardeo de Gernika* (Gernika: Gernika-Lumo, 1996), 98.

13 Testimonies of Sebastián Uria, in William Smallwood, *The Day Gernika was Bombed* (Gernika: Gernika-Lumoko udala, 2012), 36.

14 Jose Labauria, "La Roseraie," April 2, 1938, in José María Gamboa, and Jean-Claude Larronde, eds., *La guerra civil en Euzkadi: 136 testimonios inéditos recogidos por Jose Miguel de Barandiaran* (Milafranga: Bidasoa, 2005), 603.

15 Talón, *El holocausto de Guernica*, 39–40.

16 Alberto Onaindia, *Hombre de paz en la guerra* (Buenos Aires: Ekin, 1973), 238.

17 Noel Monks, *Eyewitness* (London: Frederick Muller Ltd., 1955), 94–95.

18 Joxe Iturria, *Memorias de Guerra* (Gernika: Gernika-Lumoko Udala, 2013), 75.

19 Castor Uriarte, *Bombas y mentiras sobre Guernica: acusa su arquitecto municipal cuando la guerra* (Bilbao: Gráficas Ellacuria, 1976), 64.

20 Maier, *Guernica*, 128.

21 Telegram of the Italian embassy in London, Archivio Storico Diplomatico del Ministero degli Affari Esteri [AMAE], Affari Politici (Spagna, 1931–1945), Busta 20 (1937), 19.

22 Telegram of Sir George Ogilvie-Forbes, attaché of the British embassy in Berlin, to Anthony Eden, April 29, 1937, in Medlicott and Dakin, eds., *Documents on British Foreign Policy (1919–1939)*, 688.

23 Maier, *Guernica*, 140–143.

24 James S. Corum, *Wolfram von Richthofen: Master of the German Air War* (Lawrence: University Press of Kansas, 2008), 134.

25 Data provided by José Ángel Echániz and Vicente del Palacio based on the municipal records of July 20, 1936 (5,630 inhabitants, 2,504 men and 3,126 women), in José Ángel Echániz and Vicente del Palacio, "Los muertos del bombardeo," *El Correo*, April 25, 2004. Humberto Unzueta mentions 5,729, adding the inhabitants of Gernika and the Errenteria neighborhood of Ajangiz. In Humberto Unzueta,"Gernikako bonbaketa. Hildakoak. 1937–4–26" (pamphlet printed by the author, 1992), 9.

26 500 habitants in 1644, 4.500 in 1920 and 6.000 in 1936. Gonzalo Cárdenas Rodríguez, *Datos para la reconstrucción del pueblo adoptado de Guernica {Typed text of the lecture delivered by the architect of the General*

Directorate for Devastated Regions, Gonzalo de Cárdenas Rodríguez, in the auditorium of the exhibition of the reconstruction of Spain, on July 3, 1940}, Dirección General de Regiones Devastadas y Reparaciones, Madrid, 1940, 21. Fundación Sancho el Sabio [FSS], ATV 20864. See also Gonzalo Cárdenas Rodríguez, "La Reconstrucción de Guernica," *Boletín de la Real Sociedad Vascongada de Amigos del País*, 2, no. 2 (1946): 16.

27 Ministerio de Gobernación, Dirección General de Regiones Devastadas. Comisión de Vizcaya, *Reconstrucción de la villa de Guernica. Memoria*, 1940, p. 3. Gernikako Bonbaketako Dokumentazio Zentrua [GBDZ], Regiones devastadas, Caja 1, Carp. 2 bis.

28 Jose Labauria, "La Roseraie," 602.

4 Gernika has not been bombed: It has been destroyed by fire and gasoline

1 Operazioni di Bilbao. Telegrama del general Carlo Bossi. Salamanca, April 27, 1937. AMAE, Gabinetto del Ministro (1923–1943), Busta 7 (Uffizio Spagna Leg. 44, No 1250).

2 *ABC*, April 29, 1937.

3 *Proa*, 127, April 30, 1937.

4 *Proa*, 126, April 29, 1937. It was also partially reproduced in the Euzkadi newspaper on April 28.

5 *Proa*, 126, April 29, 1937.

6 Radio Verdad. [April 28, 1937]. Archivo General Militar de Ávila [AGMA], Caja 2103, Carpeta 10/ 1.

7 Rosa Álvarez and Ramón Sala, *El cine en la zona nacional: 1936–1939* (Bilbao: Mensajero, Bilbao, 2000), 146.

8 Parte oficial faccioso. [April 29, 1937]. AGMA, Caja 2103, Carpeta 10/ 1.

9 Transmission of radio address by General Queipo de Llano about the destruction of Gernika. Report of Charles A. Bay, consul of the United States in Seville to the Secretary of State. Seville, May 3, 1937. NARA, College Park, U.S. Ambassador Claude G. Bowers Files (Files 852.00/ . . . , Boxes 3687 to 3701), Document 852.00/5410, pp. 1–4.

10 Transmission of radio address by General Queipo de Llano about the destruction of Gernika. Report of Charles A. Bay, consul of the United States in Seville to the Secretary of State. Seville, May 3, 1937. NARA, College Park, U.S. Ambassador Claude G. Bowers Files (Files 852.00/ . . . , Boxes 3687 to 3701), Document 852.00/5410, pp. 1–4.

11 Transmission of radio address by General Queipo de Llano about the destruction of Gernika. Report of Charles A. Bay, consul of the United States in Seville to the Secretary of State. Seville, May 3, 1937. NARA,

College Park, U.S. Ambassador Claude G. Bowers Files (Files 852.00/ ..., Boxes 3687 to 3701), Document 852.00/5410, pp. 1–4.

12 Situation Report No. 253. Berlin, April 29, 1937, in Maier, *Guernica*, 141–142.

13 Situation Report No. 254. Berlin, April 30, 1937, in Maier, *Guernica*, 142.

14 Maier, *Guernica*, 140–143.

15 Maier, *Guernica*, 192.

16 Maier, *Guernica*, 160–161.

17 "Las repercusiones en el extranjero por el bombardeo de Guernica," *Les Temps*, April 30, 1937, in AMTM, A03/C08/E02/D57 y D58.

18 "Las repercusiones en el extranjero por el bombardeo de Guernica."

19 "Las repercusiones en el extranjero por el bombardeo de Guernica."

20 *Información alemana*, Berlin, [early May 1937], AGMA, Caja 2103, Carpeta 10/ 1.

21 *Información alemana*, Berlin, [early May 1937], AGMA, Caja 2103, Carpeta 10/ 1.

22 "La retirada de los vascos," *The Times*, April 29, 1937, AMTM, A03/C08/E02/D57.

23 Radio Milán, Milán, [April 26, 1937], AGMA, Caja 2103, Carpeta 10/ 1.

24 "La retirada de los vascos."

25 Report by Claude G. Bowers to Cordell Hull, U.S. Secretary of State. Donibane Lohitzune, May 5, 1937. NARA, U.S. Department of State Files 1930–1939 (Files 852.00/ ..., Boxes 6386 to 6407), Document 852.00/5427. Hugo Sperrle also wrote an article on armaments and tactics of war in the special issue of the magazine of the German army Die Wehrmacht, of May 30, 1939.

26 The reporter refers to Lieutenant Friedrich-Franz Cramon, pilot of unit J/88. *Declaración prestada ante el juzgado especial decano de los de Bilbao con fecha catorce de mayo del corriente año por Joachim Hans Wandel de 23 años de edad, soltero, estudiante de ingeniero domiciliado en Breslau, Alemania*, Centro Documental de la Memoria Histórica [AHN], Salamanca, Político-Social, Carpeta 940.

27 "Los aviones que bombardearon Guernica y que actúan en el frente vasco son alemanes, conducidos por pilotos de la misma nacionalidad," *Ahora*, May 30, 1937, 8; and "El bombardeo de Guernica. Informe de la Comisión de Expertos," *ABC*, May 30, 1937, 7.

28 Letter of the Duque of Alba. London, May 1937. Fondo embajada de Londres. Legajo 248 G.1 6919. Publicaciones Duque de Alba (1937–1938). AGA.

29 Jeffrey Hart, "The Great Guernica Fraud," *National Review*, January 5, 1973, 27–29.

5 Guernica was bombed, but the destructon was mainly due to the fire

1 Xabier Irujo, "The Impact of the Bombing of Gernika in the American Press," in Sandra Ott, ed., *War, Exile, Justice, and Everyday Life, 1936–1945*, 33–57 (Reno: Center for Basque Studies Press–University of Nevada, 2011).

2 AMAE, Affari Politici (Spagna, 1931–1945), Busta 20 (1937), p. 39. GBDZ. See also, Speech by Julio Álvarez del Vayo before the Council of the League of Nations. Geneva, May 27, 1937. NARA, U.S. Department of State Files 1930–1939 (Files 852.00/ . . . , Box 6401), Document 852.00/5682.

3 Report of Lieutenant Karl von Knauer, chief of the first K/88 squad of Junkers Ju 52 that bombed Gernika, on February 6, 1974, in Maier, *Guernica*, 195.

4 Promemory. May 8, 1937. AMAE, Gabinetto del Ministro (1923–1943), Busta 1 (Uffizio Spagna No 1244), 1–3.

5 Instruction to the members of the Italian delegation at the Non-intervention Committee. AMAE, Affari Politici (Spagna, 1931–1945), Busta 19 (1937), 1–4. GBDZ.

6 Vicente Machimbarrena, "Memorias de la Escuela de Caminos. Época contemporánea del cronista," *Revista de Obras Públicas* (November 1942): 553.

7 "Bombardeo e incendio de Guernica. Sobre investigación de lo anterior. Con informe del ingeniero de minas Miláns del Bosch, sobre causas de la destrucción de dicha ciudad." Gasteiz, May 1, 1937. Archivo General Militar de Ávila [AGMA], C. 2585, Cp. 66 / 1–3.

8 "Bombardeo e incendio de Guernica."

9 "Bombardeo e incendio de Guernica."

10 "Bombardeo e incendio de Guernica."

11 "Bombardeo e incendio de Guernica."

12 "Bombardeo e incendio de Guernica."

13 "Bombardeo e incendio de Guernica."

14 "Bombardeo e incendio de Guernica."

15 *Guernica. Being the Official Report . . .* , 15.

16 *Guernica. Being the Official Report . . .* , 15–16.

17 *Guernica. Being the Official Report . . .* , 20.

18 He should not be confused with Wolfram von Richthofen, Chief of Staff of the Condor Legion and architect of the bombing of Gernika. Joachim was also an engineer, with the rank of colonel, and was attached to the General Staff of the Condor Legion for what he signed as "Richthofen 2." They were not siblings.

19 Letter from Joachim von Richthofen to General Karl F. Schweickhard of May 25, 1939. Archivo Federal de Freiburg, Archivo Militar (Bundesarchiv-Militärarchiv). Este documento me fue facilitado por el profesor Ángel Viñas.

20 Richthofen's journal entry of April 30, 1937, in Maier, *Guernica*, 128.

21 *Guernica. Being the Official Report . . .* , 49.

22 *Guernica. Being the Official Report . . .* , 37.

23 *Guernica. Being the Official Report . . .* , 12.

24 *Guernica. Being the Official Report . . .* , 4–5.

25 *Guernica. Being the Official Report . . .* , 13.

26 *Guernica. Being the Official Report . . .* , 29.

27 *Guernica. Being the Official Report . . .* , 30.

28 *Guernica. Being the Official Report . . .* , 11.

29 *Guernica. Being the Official Report . . .* , 12.

30 Maier, *Guernica*, 192.

31 Maier, *Guernica*, 195.

32 Statement of Lieutenant Karl von Knauer, head of the first K/88 squad of Junkers Ju 52 that bombed Gernika, on February 6, 1974, in Maier, *Guernica. La intervención alemana en España y el "caso Guernica,"* 194.

33 *Informe sobre la situación de las Provincias Vascongadas bajo el dominio rojo-separatista*, Universidad de Valladolid, Valladolid, 1938, p. 13.

34 *Informe sobre la situación de las Provincias Vascongadas*, 13.

35 "Guernica," *The Times*, July 9, 1969.

36 "Guernica fue destruido por los republicanos en retirada, afirma historiador inglés Crozier," *Daily Telegraph*, July 11, 1969.

37 Ricardo de la Cierva, *Historia actualizada de la Segunda República y la Guerra de España (1931–1939) con la denuncia de las patrañas* (Madrid: Fénix, 2003), 743.

38 De la Cierva, *Historia actualizada de la Segunda República y la Guerra de España*, 743.

39 Jaime Del Burgo, *Conspiración y Guerra Civil* (Madrid: Alfaguara, 1970), 861.

40 Jesús Salas, *Guernica* (Madrid: Rialp, 1987), 160.

41 Salas, *Guernica*, 161.

42 Salas, *Guernica*, 161–162.

43 Salas, *Guernica*, 162.

44 Talón, *El holocausto de Guernica*, 23.

45 Talón, *El holocausto de Guernica*, 295.

46 Talón, *El holocausto de Guernica*, 295.

47 Jorge Vilches, "Guernica. 27 toneladas de bombas en tres horas," *La Razón*, Sunday, March 5, 2017, 68.

6 Guernica was bombed, but the destructon was mainly due to the action of Italian planes

1　Maier, *Guernica*, 179.

2　Wolfram Richthofen, diary entry, April 25, 1937, 121.

3　*Efecto de los bombardeos sobre ciudades españolas (frente de Vizcaya)*. May 28, 1937. Federal Archive of Freiburg, Military Archive (Bundesarchiv-Militärarchiv). This document was provided to me by Ángel Viñas.

4　RLVB, June 9, 1937.

5　Wolfram Richthofen, diary entry, April 25, 1937, 120.

6　Maier, *Guernica*,. 179.

7　Erwin Jaenecke et al., *The German Luftwaffe in the Spanish Civil War* (Buxton: Military Library Research Service Ltd., 2006), 137–138.

7 Gernika was bombed and shelled by Basque troops

1　*Guernica. Being the Official Report . . .* , 2.

2　*Guernica. Being the Official Report . . .* , 43–44.

3　Letter from Wolfram von Richthofen to General Kindelán, signed in Burgos on August 9, 1937. The Documentation Center of the Gernika Peace Museum keeps a copy of Richthofen's report. It has been also cited by Imanol Villa, *Gernika, el bombardeo* (Bilbao: Idem4 & Expressive S.L., 2008), 93.

4　Report No. 31 of Henry Chilton, British Ambassador, to the air intelligence services. April 11, 1937. National Archives at Kew [NAK], HW 22/1.

8 It was a strategic bombing whose objective was the Errenteria bridge

1　Ángel Viñas, Epílogo [to the new edition of Herbert Southworth's work on the bombing of Gernika], manuscript, 42. See also the Italian reports: *Attivitá Giornalera dell'Aviazione Legionaria del Continente dal Luglio 1936 al Dicembre 1937. Volumen 1*, Ufficio Storico dell'Aeronautica Militare [USAM], Busta 70, Fascicolo 7. Y, *Ordine d'operazione n.º 48*, Soria, 26 de April de 1937. *Diario Storico*, USAM, Busta 68, Fascicolo 98.

2　Rolf-Dieter Müller, *La muerte caída del cielo. Historia de los bombardeos durante la Segunda Guerra Mundial* (Barcelona: Ediciones Destino, 2008), 54.

3　Corum, *Wolfram von Richthofen*, 134.

4　Telegram from Franco to Sperrle, Salamanca, May 7, 1937. AGMA, C. 2585, Cp. 66 / 6.

5　Maier, *Guernica*, 181.

6 Talón, *El holocausto de Guernica*, 53–57. Corum, *Wolfram von Richthofen*, 21 and 134–137. Müller, *La muerte caída del cielo*, 54–55.

7 Müller, *La muerte caída del cielo*, 50–55.

8 Adolf Galland, *Memorias. Los primeros y los últimos* (Barcelona: Editorial EHR, 1955), 53–54.

9 Villa, *Gernika, el bombardeo*, 94.

10 Interview with Pete T. Cenarrusa. Boise (Idaho), Monday, April 18, 2010, and Thursday, November 11, 2010.

11 According to Castor Uriarte, municipal architect of Gernika in 1937, the Errenteria bridge was exactly 19.5 meters long and 9.5 meters wide. Uriarte, *Bombas y mentiras sobre Guernica: acusa su arquitecto municipal cuando la guerra* (Bilbao: Gráficas Ellacuria, 1976), 44. The three interviews were held in Boise, Idaho, between November 8 and 10, 2010.

12 Müller, *La muerte caída del cielo*, 54.

13 It has been documented that more than two-thirds of the bombs were incendiary.

14 The destruction of 85.5 percent of the buildings in town is now documented.

15 Xabier Irujo, *On Basque Politics. Conversations with Pete Cenarrusa* (Brussels: EURI, 2011), 138.

16 *Yearbook of the German Aviation*, 1938, 138. National Archives Collection of Foreign Records Seized (Record Group 242). Captured German Records NARA, Records of Headquarters, German Air Force High Command (Oberkommando der Luftwaffe/OKL). Microfilm Publication T321, R. 105.

17 Interview with Pete T. Cenarrusa. Boise (Idaho), Monday, April 18, 2010, and Thursday, November 11, 2010.

18 Salas bases its data on the Herrán Report, which lacks credibility. Salas, *Guernica*, 158.

19 Interview with Pete T. Cenarrusa. Boise (Idaho), Monday, April 18, 2010, and Thursday, November 11, 2010.

20 *Auswertung Rügen*. Viñas uses the *Heft 2, Führung, Abschnitte IV bis VI*, file RL 7/57b. Viñas, *Epílogo*, 58.

21 Villa, *Gernika, el bombardeo*, 94.

22 Testimony of Castor Uriarte, in Smallwood, *The Day Gernika Was Bombed*, 107–108. A councilor from Gernika interviewed by a correspondent of the French newspaper *L'Humanité* said that despite the level of material destruction, none of the military objectives themselves were achieved. At the same time, the houses of recognized Francoists or Carlists of the town, such as the house of the Count of Montefuerte, the notary Aurelio Ortiz, the houses of Andrés and Juan Allende Salazar, and those of the Herránz, Herrán, Arana, Enderika, Santo Domingo, and Loizaga families, remained

untouched. Paul Vaillant-Couturier affirmed that neither the businesses nor the houses of the families affected by the regime, such as those of Carlos Santo Domingo and his brother-in-law Enderika, or the villa of Herrán, the house of the notary Ortiz, the palace of the count of Montefuerte, were demolished. In "Demain, Bilbao," *L'Humanité*, May 13, 1937, 1–3; and "Gernika'ren errausketa," *Euzko Deya*, September 12, 1937, 4.

9 It was a strategic bombing whose objective was to cut the withdrawal to the Basque troops

1 Maier, *Guernica*, 143.

2 Salas, *Guernica*, 117.

3 Wolfram von Richthofen, diary entry, April 26, 1937, in Maier, *Guernica*, 121.

4 Maier, *Guernica*, 182.

5 Orden de operaciones de las brigadas 1 y 4. Gasteiz, April 25, 1937. GBDZ.

6 Operazioni Fronte Nord. Informe del general Doria (Bastico) al conde Galeazzo Ciano. May 3, 1937. AMAE, Gabinetto del Ministro (1923–1943), Busta 1 (Uffizio Spagna No 1244), pp. 1–10.

7 Vincenzo Velardi, *Promemoria per S. E. Il Sottosecretario de Stato*, Gasteiz, May 6, 1937, p. 5, in USAM, Busta 76, Fascicolo 14.

8 Maier, *Guernica*, 121.

9 The distance between Arta and Gernika is around 22 kilometers.

10 Wolfram von Richthofen, diary entry, April 27, 1937, in Maier, *Guernica*, 124.

11 Pierre Hericourt, "La liberation de l'éspagne," [Paris], [May 1937]. AMTM, A08/C07/E05/P61/P02.

12 Luis M. Jimenez de Aberasturi and Juan C. Jimenez de Aberasturi, *La guerra en Euskadi* (Donostia: Txertoa, 2007), 68. See also, Talón, *El holocausto de Guernica* (Barcelona: Plaza & Janés, 1987), 40.

13 Report on the service trip of Colonel Jaenecke. May 18, 1937. In Maier, *Guernica*, 180.

14 Report of the service trip of Colonel Meise. March 21, 1938. In Maier, *Guernica*, 181.

15 Corum, *Wolfram von Richthofen*, 135–136.

16 Maier, *Guernica*, 182.

17 Maier, *Guernica*, 191–192.

18 Corum, *Wolfram von Richthofen*, 134.

19 Talón, *El holocausto de Guernica*, 46.

20 Salas, *Guernica*, 117.

21 Salas, *Guernica*, 140.

22 In order to capture the Basque troops in retreat, the Spanish troops would have had to advance between 20 and 30 times faster than the daily average advance to that date. The Spanish troops were advancing about 0.5 miles per day, and this operation required an advance of 10 to 15 miles in one single day.

23 Salas, *Guernica*, 117.

10 Gernika was a legitimate military objective because . . .

1 Letter from Richthofen to General Kindelan on the situation of the troops in the Bizkaian front and the bombing of Gernika, August 9, 1937. Archivo Histórico del Ejército del Aire de Villaviciosa de Odón [AHEA], 958/3.

2 Telegram from Franco to Spcrrlc, Salamanca, May 7, 1937. AGMA, C. 2585, Cp. 66 / 6.

3 Maier, *Guernica*, 192.

4 See both documents in Maier, *Guernica*, 140–143.

5 Testimony of Corrado Ricci, in Talón, *El holocausto de Guernica*, 149.

6 Talón, *El holocausto de Guernica*, 45.

7 Salas, *Guernica*, 24.

8 Corum, *Wolfram von Richthofen*, 134.

9 Some authors have referred to "barracks of Gernika" implying that they were "posts or sites where the army was stationed in the campaign." This is not the case. The buildings designated for use by the Basque army were not used to plan war operations, nor did the general staff lodge there; rather, they were designated for the rest of troops that were out of duty or to soldiers who had left the hospital and needed some rest.

10 AMAE, Gabinetto del Ministro (1923–1943), Busta 7 (Uffizio Spagna Leg. 44, No 1250).

11 "Bombardeo e incendio de Guernica," 1–3.

12 "Los facciosos bombardean, a sabiendas, los hospitales," *El Liberal*, 36, no. 12.429 (October 28, 1936): 2.

13 "La guerra en los frentes de Guipúzcoa," *El Noticiero Bilbaino*, 62, no. 21.376 (October 28, 1936): 1.

14 Müller, *La muerte caída del cielo,* 55.

15 "Bombardeo e incendio de Guernica," 1–3.

11 It was not a terror bombing

1 Müller, *La muerte caída del cielo*, 54.

2 Corum, *Wolfram von Richthofen*, 136.

3 Wolfram von Richthofen, diary entry, April 2, 1937, in Maier, *Guernica*, 101–102.

4 Corum, *Wolfram von Richthofen*, 22–23.

5 Corum, *Wolfram von Richthofen*, 135.

6 Wolfram von Richthofen, diary entry, April 2, 1937, in Maier, *Guernica*, 98.

7 Wolfram von Richthofen, diary entry, April 2, 1937, in Maier, *Guernica*, 124.

8 Wolfram von Richthofen, diary entry, April 2, 1937, in Maier, *Guernica*, 130.

9 Wolfram von Richthofen, diary entry, April 2, 1937, in Maier, *Guernica*, 130.

10 *Efecto de los bombardeos sobre ciudades españolas (frente de Vizcaya)*, May 28, 1937.

11 "Dopo aver affermato che la pressa di Bilbao si presentava difficile e durissima salvo che non si fosse prodotto il collasso morale delle troppe," *Oggetto: Offensiva su Bilbao*, USAM, Leg. 97.

12 Velardi, *Promemoria per S. E. Il Sottosegretario di Stato*, 6.

13 Telegram from Benito Mussolini to General Ettore Bastico, Rome, June 21, 1937. AMAE, Gabinetto del Ministro (1923–1943), Busta 7 (Uffizio Spagna Leg. 44, No 1250).

14 Maier, *Guernica*, 132.

12 The destruction was mainly due to the mismanagement of the Basque firefighters

1 *Guernica. Being the Official Report . . .* , 24.

2 *Guernica. Being the Official Report . . .* , 25–26.

3 *Guernica. Being the Official Report . . .* , 27.

4 *Guernica. Being the Official Report . . .* , 28.

5 *Guernica. Being the Official Report . . .* , 41.

6 *Guernica. Being the Official Report . . .* , 10.

7 Salas, *Guernica*, 35.

8 Salas, *Guernica*, 162.

9 Ferdinando Raffaelli, diary entry, in Talón, *El holocausto de Guernica*, 148.

10 Morning session of the day 82, Friday, March 15, 1946.*Trial of the Major War Criminals Before the International Military Tribunal, Nuremberg, 14 November 1945–1 October 1946: Proceedings*, International Military Tribunal, [Washington D.C.], 1947, vol. 9, p. 133.

11 Smallwood, *The Day Guernica was Bombed*.

13 Franco did not know anything

1 *Guernica. Being the Official Report . . .* , 15–16.
2 *Proa*, 126, April 29, 1937.
3 José E. Díez, ed., *Colección de proclamas y arengas del excelentísimo señor general don Francisco Franco, jefe del Estado y generalísimo del ejército salvador de España* (Seville: M. Carmona, 1937), 219.
4 Maier, *Guernica*, 150–151.
5 Talón, *El holocausto de Guernica*, 73.
6 José Manuel Martínez Bande, *La Invasión de Aragón y el desembarco en Mallorca* (Madrid: San Martín, 1970), 72.
7 Talón, *El holocausto de Guernica*, 79.
8 Müller, *La muerte caída del cielo*, 54.
9 Jaenecke et al., *The German Luftwaffe in the Spanish Civil War*, 137–138.
10 Maier, *Guernica*, 179.
11 Corum, *Wolfram von Richthofen*, 136.
12 Ricardo de la Cierva, "La polémica y la verdad sobre Guernica," *La historia se confiesa* 45 (1976): 285.
13 Salas, *Guernica*, 185.
14 Instrucciones generales para el enlace con la aviación, Salamanca, November 17, 1936. AHEA, A-2187/55.
15 Salas, *Guernica*, 187.
16 Telegram from Franco to Sperrle, Salamanca, May 7, 1937. AGMA, C. 2585, Cp. 66 / 6.
17 Letter from Richthofen to Kindelan about the situation of the troops in the Bizcaian front and the bombing of Gernika. August 9, 1937. AHEA, 958/3. See also, Ángel Viñas, "Epílogo [to the new edition of Herbert Southworth's work on the bombing of Gernika]," manuscript, 38.
18 Letter from Richthofen to Kindelan.
19 Ricardo de la Cierva, "Guernica: Los documentos contra el mito," *Nueva y definitiva historia de la Guerra Civil* (Madrid: Época coleccionables, 1986), 487.
20 Wolfram von Richthofen, diary entry, March 26, 1937, in Maier, *Guernica*, 93.

14 Spanish aircraft did not participate in the bombing

1 De la Cierva, *Historia actualizada de la Segunda República y la Guerra de España (1931–1939)*, 741.
2 Salas, *Guernica*, 155–157.
3 Talón, *El holocausto de Guernica*, 133–151.
4 Salas, *Guernica*, 155–156.
5 Salas, *Guernica*, 156.

15 It was an accident

1 Galland, *Memorias*, 53–54.

2 *Guernica. Being the Official Report . . .* , 4–5.

3 Corum, *Wolfram von Richthofen*, 136.

4 Report of the service trip of Colonel Meise, March 21, 1938, in Maier, *Guernica*, 181.

5 Report of the service trip of Colonel Jaenecke, May 18, 1937, in Maier, *Guernica*, 180.

6 Müller, *La muerte caída del cielo*, 53.

7 Wolfram von Richthofen, diary entry, March 26, 1937, in Maier, *Guernica*, 104.

8 *Efecto de los bombardeos sobre ciudades españolas (frente de Vizcaya)*, May 28, 1937.

9 Peter C. Smith, *Stuka Spearhead: The Lightning War from Poland to Dunkirk, 1939–1940* (Barnsley, South Yorkshire: Pen & Sword Aviation, 2015), 6–7.

10 John Weal, *Luftwaffe Schlachtgruppen* (Oxford: Osprey Publishing Ltd., Oxford, 2013), 8.

11 Nigel Askey, *Operation Barbarossa: The complete organisational and statistical analysis* (self-pub., 2013), 129.

12 Jean D. Lepage, *Aircraft of the Luftwaffe, 1935–1945: An Illustrated Guide* (Jefferson, NC: McFarland & Co., 2009), 114.

13 Dennis Showalter, *Hitler's Panzers: The Lightning Attacks that Revolutionized Warfare* (New York: Berkley Books, 2014).

14 Corum, *Wolfram von Richthofen*, 166.

15 Weal, *Luftwaffe Schlachtgruppen*, 19–20.

16 Corum, *Wolfram von Richthofen*, 168.

17 Doug Dildy, *Fall Gelb 1940 (2): Airborne Assault on the Low Countries* (Oxford: Osprey Publishing, 2015), 61.

18 Henry L. De Zeng and Douglas G. Stankey, *Dive-bomber and Ground-Attack Units of the Luftwaffe 1933–1945: A Reference Source* (Hersham, 2009), 175.

19 Interview of Pete T. Cenarrusa, Boise (Idaho), Monday, April 18, 2010, and Thursday, November 11, 2010.

20 Telegram from Franco to Sperrle, Salamanca, May 7, 1937. AGMA, C. 2585, Cp. 66 / 6.

21 Letter from Richthofen to Kindelán, signed in Burgos on August 9, 1937. GBDZ.

22 Maier, *Guernica*, 189.

23 Maier, *Guernica*, 192.

24 Maier, *Guernica*, 192.

25 Letter from Ehrhart K. Dellmensingen to Edu Neumann, August 3, 1983, in Salas, *Guernica*, 280.

26 Salas, *Guernica*, 148–150.

27 Müller, *La muerte caída del cielo*, 54–55.

28 *Ordine d'operazione n.º 48*, Soria, 26 de April de 1937. *Diario Storico*, USAM, Busta 68, Fascicolo 98.

29 Yvonne Cloud (Yvonne Kapp) and Richard Ellis, *The Basque Children in England. An Account of their Life at North Stoneham Camp* (London: Victor Gollancz Ltd., 1937), 56–57.

16 Richthofen ordered his men to spare Gernika and to throw bombs as a signal

1 Maier, *Guernica*, 189.

2 *Ordine d'operazione No. 48*. Diario Storico, USAM, Busta 68, Fascicolo 98. Also published by Salas in *Guernica*, 189 and annex 30.

3 Smallwood, *The Day Guernica Was Bombed*, 51–58.

4 *Proa*, 126, April 29, 1937.

5 Salas, *Guernica*, 187.

6 Xabier Irujo, "Bombardeos en Euskadi (1936–1937)," unpublished manuscript. See an extract of this work in Joseba Agirreazkuenaga and Mikel Urkijo, eds., *Senderos de la memoria. Relación de espacios vinculados a la memoria de la guerra civil y el exilio* (Leioa: Grupo de Investigación Biography & Parliament de la Universidad del País Vasco, 2016), 2: 177–228.

7 Letter from Richthofen to Kindelan.

8 Letter from Richthofen to Kindelan.

9 Maier, *Guernica*, 52.

10 Irujo, *Bombardeos en Euskadi (1936–1937)*.

17 Nine, 39, or 43 aircraft participated in the bombing

1 Maier, *Guernica*, 189.

2 *Guernica. Being the Official Report . . .* , 28.

3 *Guernica. Being the Official Report . . .* , 37.

4 Maier, *Guernica*, 195.

5 Maier, *Guernica*, 192.

6 Salas, *Guernica*, 150 and 153.

7 Corum, *Wolfram von Richthofen*, 134.

8 Müller, *La muerte caída del cielo. Historia de los bombardeos durante la Segunda Guerra Mundial*, 54.

9 Talón, *El holocausto de Guernica*, 134.

10 For a detailed examination of the fighter planes and bombers that

participated in the bombing see Xabier Irujo, *El Gernika de Richthofen. Un ensayo de bombardeo de terror* (Gernika: Gernikako Bakearen Museoa Fundazioa/Gernika-Lumoko Udala, 2012), 548–555.

11 Maier, *Guernica*, 191.
12 Talón, *El holocausto de Guernica*, 134.
13 Maier, *Guernica*, 138.

18 Eight or 28 tons of bombs were dropped

1 Maier, *Guernica*, 189.
2 *Efecto de los bombardeos sobre ciudades españolas (frente de Vizcaya)*, May 28, 1937.
3 Letter from Richthofen to Kindelan.
4 Maier, *Guernica*, 195.
5 Corum, *Wolfram von Richthofen*, 134.
6 De la Cierva, *Historia actualizada de la Segunda República y la Guerra de España (1931–1939)*, 735.
7 Salas, *Guernica*, 157.
8 Salas, *Guernica*, 145.
9 See Xabier Irujo, *Gernika, 26 de abril de 1937* (Barcelona: Crítica, 2017), 175.
10 For a detailed description see Irujo, *El Gernika de Richthofen*, 556–558. See also Irujo, *Gernika, 26 de abril de 1937*, 176.
11 Irujo, *Gernika, 26 de abril de 1937*, 136.

19 Gernika was bombed at 1,500, 2,300, 3,500, 3,600, and 3,800 meters of altitude

1 Maier, *Guernica*, 189.
2 Maier, *Guernica*, 191.
3 Maier, *Guernica*, 195.
4 *Ordine d'operazione n.º 48*, Soria, 26 de April de 1937. *Diario Storico*, USAM, Busta 68, Fascicolo 98.
5 Villa, *Gernika, el bombardeo*, 94.
6 Ferdinando Raffaelli, *Bombardamento. Quistionario*, Ufficio di Stato Maggiore della Regia Aeronautica, Aviazione Legionaria 21° Stormo B. T., 1. Corrado Corradino, *Bombardamento. Quistionario*, Ufficio di Stato Maggiore della Regia Aeronautica, Aviazione Legionaria 24° Stormo B. T., P. 5.
7 Raffaelli, *Bombardamento. Quistionario*, 1.
8 Meteorological report of the Igeldo observatory. Bilbao, April 26, 1937.
9 Excerpt from the war diary of the observer Lieutenant Angel Seibane, Zaragoza, March 1972. AHEA, A-2125.

10 Letter from Richthofen to Karl F. Schweickhard of May 25, 1939. Archivo Federal de Freiburg, Archivo Militar (Bundesarchiv-Militärarchiv).

11 *Efecto de los bombardeos sobre ciudades españolas (frente de Vizcaya)*, May 28, 1937.

12 Testimony of Jose Ramon Urtiaga, in Smallwood, *The Day Gernika Was Bombed* (Gernika: Gernika-Lumoko udala, 2012), 53.

13 Testimonies of Pedro Gezuraga, Aurelio Artetxe, Iñaki Rezabal, and Faustino Pastor, in Smallwood, *The Day Gernika Was Bombed*, 46, 53–54, 58, and 60–61.

14 De la Cierva, *Historia actualizada de la Segunda República y la Guerra de España (1931–1939)*, 735.

15 Villa, *Gernika, el bombardeo*, 94.

16 Villa, *Gernika, el bombardeo*, 97.

20 Seventy-one percent of the city was destroyed

1 *Guernica. Being the Official Report . . .* , 16.

2 *Guernica. Being the Official Report . . .* , 14.

3 *Guernica. Being the Official Report . . .* , 15.

4 *Guernica. Being the Official Report . . .* , 45.

5 *Guernica. Being the Official Report . . .* , 14 and 16. See also Herbert R. Southworth, *Guernica! Guernica!: A Study of Journalism, Diplomacy, Propaganda and History* (Berkeley and Los Angeles: University of California Press, 1977), 356.

6 De la Cierva, *Historia actualizada de la Segunda República y la Guerra de España (1931–1939)*, 741.

7 Corum, *Wolfram von Richthofen*, 134.

8 Talón, *El holocausto de Guernica*, 25.

9 Salas, *Guernica*, 163.

10 Gonzalo Cárdenas Rodríguez, *Datos para la reconstrucción del pueblo adoptado de Guernica {Typed text of the lecture delivered by the architect of the General Directorate for Devastated Regions, Gonzalo de Cárdenas Rodríguez, in the auditorium of the exhibition of the reconstruction of Spain, on July 3, 1940}* (Madrid: Dirección General de Regiones Devastadas y Reparaciones, 1940), 29–30. FSS, ATV 20864.

21 Forty-five people died in the Andra Mari shelter

1 Maier, *Guernica*, 128.

2 *Efecto de los bombardeos sobre ciudades españolas (frente de Vizcaya)*, May 28, 1937.

3 Jose Labauria, "La Roseraie," 604. Interview with Joxe Iturria. Lesaka, May 17 and 21, June 7 and July 30, 2013. See also Joxe Iturria, *Memorias de*

Guerra (Gernika: Gernika-Lumoko udala, 2013), 78. Testimony of María Medinabeitia, Baiona, August 30, 1937, in Gamboa and Larronde, eds., *La guerra civil en Euzkadi: 136 testimonios inéditos recogidos por José Miguel de Barandiarán*, 173.

4 Interview of William Smallwood with Francisca Arriaga, 1972. WSA [William Smallwood Archive], File Gernika, E. Francisca Arriaga, 1972. Interview of William Smallwood to Kaxtor Amunarriz, 1972. WSA, File Gernika, E. Kaxtor Amunarriz, 1972. Testimony of José Ramón Urtiaga and Carmen Zabaljauregi in William Smallwood, manuscript, 1972, 50 and 67.

5 Testimony of Federico Iraeta in Smallwood, *The Day Gernika Was Bombed*, 123.

6 *Efecto de los bombardeos sobre ciudades españolas (frente de Vizcaya)*, May 28, 1937.

7 *Guernica. Being the Official Report . . .* , 24.

8 *Guernica. Being the Official Report . . .* , 8.

9 Ministerio de Gobernación. Dirección General de Regiones Devastadas. Comisión de Vizcaya, *Desescombro de Guernica*, Bilbao, 24 de December 1941, p. 1. GBDZ, Regiones Devastadas, Caja 3, Carp. 1. See also, Ángel B. Puente, *Reconstrucción de Guernica, Munguía, Maruri, Gatica, Bilbao*, 1941, p. 19. FSS, ATV 6453.

10 The authors of the report included Felipe Bastarrechea among the victims of the said shelter, and it is well documented that he did not die there.

11 *Guernica. Being the Official Report . . .* , 51–53.

12 *Guernica. Being the Official Report . . .* , 8.

13 *Efecto de los bombardeos sobre ciudades españolas (frente de Vizcaya)*, May 28, 1937.

14 *Efecto de los bombardeos sobre ciudades españolas (frente de Vizcaya)*, May 28, 1937.

15 *Guernica. Being the Official Report . . .* , 7.

16 *Guernica. Being the Official Report . . .* , 7.

17 *Guernica. Being the Official Report . . .* , 7.

18 Interview of William Smallwood with Castor Uriarte. Labastida, June 6, 1972. WSA, File Gernika, E. Castor Uriarte, 1972.

19 Talón, *El holocausto de Guernica*, 42.

20 *Guernica. Being the Official Report . . .* , 24.

21 Salas, *Guernica*, 196.

22 Salas, *Guernica*, 165–167.

23 Salas, *Guernica*, 195.

22 One hundred and twenty-six people died in the bombing

1 Noel Monks, "Guernica Destroyed by German Planes, 26 April 1937," in *Eyewitness* (London: Frederick Muller Ltd., 1955), 97. See also John Carey, ed., *Eyewitness to History* (Cambridge, Mass.: Harvard University Press, 1987), 519–521.

2 George L. Steer, *The Tree of Gernika: A Field Study of Modern War* (London: Hodder and Stoughton, London, 1938), chapter XX.

3 Mathieu Corman, *¡Salud camarada! Cinq mois sur les fronts d'Espagne* (Paris: Editions Tribord, Paris, 1937), 285.

4 Alberto Onaindia, *Capítulos de mi vida I. Hombre de paz en la guerra* (Buenos Aires: Ekin, 1973), 240.

5 *Relación de víctimas causadas por la aviación facciosa en sus incursiones del mes de abril de 1937*, Eusko Jaurlaritzaren Artxibo eta Dokumentu Ondarearen Zerbitzua (IRARGI), Doc. GE-0037-03.

6 Noel Monks, *Eyewitness* (London: Frederick Muller Ltd., 1955), 99.

7 Noel Monks, "I Saw the German Planes Bomb Guernica," *Daily Express*, May 1, 1937, 10. *Foreign Wings over the Basque Country* (London: The Friends of Spain, 1937), 41.

8 Monks, "I Saw the German Planes Bomb Guernica."

9 Monks, "I Saw the German Planes Bomb Guernica," 10. *Foreign Wings over the Basque Country*, 41. See also "El yo acuso de un periodista inglés," *Tierra Vasca*, May 18, 1937, 1.

10 *El Liberal*, April 30, 1937.

11 Albert Onaindia, "A priest's account," *The Times*, May 3, 1937.

12 For a detailed description of the witnesses see Irujo, *El Gernika de Richthofen*, 262–268.

13 For a detailed study of the calculation of fatalities see Irujo, *El Gernika de Richthofen*, 257–336. See also Irujo, *Gernika, 26 de abril de 1937*, 181–201.

14 Errenteria had 500 habitants in 1936 and 535 in 1940. Unzueta, "Gernikako bonbaketa," 10.

15 Telegram of the Italian Embassy in London. AMAE, Affari Politici (Spagna, 1931–1945), Busta 20 (1937), p. 19.

16 *Guernica. Being the Official Report . . .* , 15.

17 *Guernica. Being the Official Report . . . ,* 41–42.

18 *Guernica. Being the Official Report . . . ,* 51.

19 *Guernica. Being the Official Report . . . ,* 51–53.

20 Testimony of Pedro Agirre, in Smallwood, *The Day Gernika Was Bombed*, 125–126.

21 Ministerio de Gobernación. Dirección General de Regiones Devastadas. Comisión de Vizcaya, *Desescombro de Guernica*, Bilbao, December 24, 1941, p. 1. GBDZ, Regiones Devastadas, Caja 3, Carp. 1. See also Ángel B.

Puente, *Reconstrucción de Guernica, Munguía, Maruri, Gatica, Bilbao*, 1941, p. 19. FSS, ATV 6453.

22 *Guernica. Being the Official Report . . .* , 14.

23 Talón, *El holocausto de Guernica*, 38.

24 Pedro Pascual, "La Guerra del 36, su historia y su circunstancia," *Arriba*, January 31, 1970.

25 Corum, *Wolfram von Richthofen*, 21.

26 Talón, *El holocausto de Guernica*, 33–37.

27 Unzueta, "Gernikako bonbaketa," 21–22. See also Humberto Unzueta, "Los muertos inoportunos," *Aldaba Gernika-Lumoko Aldizkaria*, 86 (March–April), 1997: 42.

28 AA.VV., *Sustrai Erreak 2, Guernica 1937* (Gernika-Lumo: Aldaba-Gernikazarra, Gernika-Lumo, 2012), 331.

29 Salas, *Guernica*, 36–37 and 163–167.

30 Corum, *Wolfram von Richthofen*, 136–137.

23 Witnesses lie and exaggerate

1 *Guernica. Being the Official Report . . .* , 3–4.

2 Martha C. Howell and Walter Prevenier, *From Reliable Sources: An Introduction to Historical Methods* (Ithaca: Cornell University Press, 2001), 69–85.

3 Irujo, *El Gernika de Richthofen*, 258–259. See also Howell and Prevenier, *From Reliable Sources,* 69–85.

4 Gilbert J. Garraghan, *A Guide to Historical Method* (New York: Fordham University Press, 1946). See also Robert J. Shafer, ed., *A Guide to Historical Method* (Chicago: Dorsey Press, 1980).

24 We are not monsters . . .

1 First version of the report of the military section of the air force. In Maier, *Guernica*, 188.

2 Jaenecke et al., *The German Luftwaffe in the Spanish Civil War*, 137–138. It is true, of course, that the pilots who committed that atrocity could have been of any other nationality, and that it is not because they were Germans that they did what they did. It is also obvious that the National-Socialist (Nazi) regime pushed these men to commit some of the worst atrocities of the 20th century, not because it is a German regime, but because it was National-Socialist.

3 Sönke Neitzel and Harald Welzer, eds., *Soldaten: On Fighting, Killing, and Dying. The Secret World War II Transcripts of German POWs* (Minneapolis: HighBridge, 2012), 45.

4   Neitzel and Welzer, *Soldados del Tercer Reich: testimonios de lucha, muerte y crimen*, 44.
5   Neitzel and Welzer, *Soldados del Tercer Reich*, 63.
6   Neitzel and Welzer, *Soldados del Tercer Reich*, 44.
7   Neitzel and Welzer, *Soldados del Tercer Reich*, 65.
8   Monks, *Eyewitness*, 99.

25 We are the real victims . . .

1   Telegram from Joachim von Ribbentrop, German ambassador in London, to the Ministry of Foreign Affairs in Berlin. London, May 4, 1937, in Maier, *Guernica*, 154.
2   Telegram from Franco to Sperrle, Salamanca, May 7, 1937. AGMA, C. 2585, Cp. 66 / 6.
3   War diary of the commander of the observation forces, Rear Admiral Boehm, entry of May 13, 1937, in Maier, *Guernica*, 146.
4   Maier, *Guernica*, 189.
5   Maier, *Guernica*, 191.
6   Maier, *Guernica*, 192.
7   *Guernica. Being the Official Report . . .* , 14.
8   *Guernica. Being the Official Report . . .* , 16.
9   Galland, *Memorias*, 53–54.
10 Müller, *La muerte caída del cielo*, 54.
11 Talón, *El holocausto de Guernica*, 38.
12 Testimony of Maria Olabarria, 52 years of age, in Paul Vaillant-Couturier, "La madre que vio morir a dos hijas," *La Voz*, May 26, 1937, 1–4, and, "Más relatos impresionantes sobre la saña y la crueldad con que procedieron los rebeldes españoles en Guernica," *El Sol*, May 27, 1937, 2. In the original French, "Demain, Bilbao," *L'Humanité*, May 13, 1937, 1–3.
13 Testimony of Juan Sistiaga, in Smallwood, *The Day Gernika Was Bombed*, 66–67.

26 The bombing of Gernika is a myth

1   De la Cierva, *Historia actualizada de la Segunda República y la Guerra de España (1931–1939)*, 727–728.
2   Talón, *El holocausto de Guernica*, 225.
3   Testimony of María Abascal, in William Smallwood, *El día en que Gernika fue bombardeada* (Gernika: Gernika-Lumoko udala, 2013), 73.
4   Testimony of Joseba Elosegi, in Smallwood, *El día en que Gernika fue bombardeada*, 79.
5   Noel Monks, "Guernica Destroyed by German Planes, 26 April 1937," in

Monks, *Eyewitness* (London: Frederick Muller Ltd., 1955), 97. See also Carey, *Eyewitness to History*, 519–521.

6 *Guernica. To Civilized Mankind* (Bilbao, 1937).

7 Testimony of Alberto Onaindia, in Smallwood, *El día en que Gernika fue bombardeada*, 76.

8 Testimony collected by Hilari Raguer from the unpublished memoirs of Aita Patxi, "En Euzkadi. Mi odisea pasionista," 223. Quoted in Raguer, *Aita Patxi. Prisionero con los gudaris* (Barcelona: Claret, 2006), 117. See also José Ignacio Lopategui, *Aita Patxi. Testimonio. 1ª parte: En la guerra (1937–1939)* (Bilbao, 1978), 63.

9 Corum, *Wolfram von Richthofen*, 134.

10 Corum, *Wolfram von Richthofen*, 134–135.

11 Joseba Agirreazkuenaga and Mikel Urkijo, eds., *Senderos de la memoria. Relación de espacios vinculados a la memoria de la guerra civil y el exilio* (Leioa: Grupo de Investigación Biography & Parliament de la Universidad del País Vasco, 2016), 2: 177–228.

12 Corum, *Wolfram von Richthofen*, 137.

27 The bombing of Gernika was not a crime

1 Corum, *Wolfram von Richthofen*, 26.

2 Müller, *La muerte caída del cielo*, 54.

3 *La intervención de Alemania a favor de Franco en las operaciones del territorio vasco*, Gobierno de Euskadi, Bilbao, 1937. See also *Texto íntegro del escrito presentado por el presidente del gobierno vasco, Sr. Aguirre, al Tribunal Militar de Nuremberg*, Paris, December 27, 1947, p. 5. EAA, LIAB-12-5.

28 If it were not for Picasso . . .

1 Telegram from Joachim von Ribbentrop, German ambassador in London, to the Ministry of Foreign Affairs in Berlin. London, May 4, 1937, in Maier, *Guernica*, 153.

2 Talón, *El holocausto de Guernica*, 198 and 214.

3 Müller, *La muerte caída del cielo. Historia de los bombardeos durante la Segunda Guerra Mundial*, 54.

4 On the impact that the bombing of Gernika had on the American press see Xabier Irujo Ametzaga, "The Impact of the Bombing of Gernika in the North American Press," in Ott, ed., *War, Exile, Justice, and Everyday Life, 1936–1946*, 33–57.

5 Survey conducted by the author through *Newspaper Archive, Access World News, Times Digital Archive, ProQuest Historical Newspapers, LexisNexis Congressional* and other secondary databases.

6   *Foreign Wings over the Basque Country.*

29 Franco Savior, Franco Merciful, Franco Architect of Peace

1   Dirección General de Regiones Devastadas y Reparaciones. Comisión de Vizcaya, *Ayuntamiento adoptado de Guernica. Relación de edificios de carácter público destruidos por acción de guerra, formulada en cumplimiento de la orden de 7 de octubre de 1939, año de la victoria*, Bilbao, November 10, 1939, pp. 31–32.

2   Boletín Oficial del Estado, No. 274, October 1, 1939, pp. 5489–5490.

3   Boletín Oficial del Estado, No. 274, October 1, 1939, pp. 5489–5490.

4   Cárdenas Rodríguez, *Datos para la reconstrucción del pueblo adoptado de Guernica*, 41.

5   "Guernica," *Revista Reconstrucción*, [s/e], [s/f], p. 6.

Epilogue: Passion for Ignorance

1   De la Cierva, *Historia actualizada de la Segunda República y la Guerra de España (1931–1939)*, 14–39.

2   Vilches, "Guernica," 68.

3   Talón, *El holocausto de Guernica*, 82.

4   Talón, *El holocausto de Guernica*, 81.

Bibliography

AA.VV. *Sustrai Erreak 2, Guernica 1937*. Gernika-Lumo: Aldaba-Gernikazarra, 2012.

Aguirre Lekube, Jose Antonio. *Escape vía Berlin. Eluding Franco in Hitler's Europe* [introduction and notes by Robert P. Clark]. Reno: University of Nevada Press, 1991.

Álvarez, Rosa, and Ramón Sala. *El cine en la zona nacional: 1936–1939*. Bilbao: Mensajero, 2000.

Astigarraga Larrañaga, Andoni de (Astilarra). *Guernica en Elosegui*. Buenos Aires: F.E.V.A., 1972.

Atxaga, Bernardo. *De Gernika a Guernica*. Barcelona: Ediciones de la Central, 2007.

Basaldua, Pedro. *En defensa de la verdad (Refutación a Mons. Franceschi)*. Buenos Aires: Ekin, 1956.

The Basque Country and the European Peace: An Analysis of German Domination of Euzkadi. London: Government of Euzkadi, 1937.

The Bombardment of Open Towns. What is a Military Objective? Is this a Military Objective? Spanish Press Services, 1938.

Bombardeo e incendio de Guernica. Sobre investigación de lo anterior. Con informe del ingeniero de minas Miláns del Bosch, sobre causas de la destrucción de dicha ciudad. Gasteiz, May 1, 1937.

Bowers, Claude. *My Mission to Spain*. New York: Simon and Schuster, 1954.

Cárdenas Rodríguez, Gonzalo. *Datos para la reconstrucción del pueblo adoptado de Guernica* [Typed text of the lecture delivered by the architect of the General Directorate for Devastated Regions, Gonzalo de Cárdenas Rodríguez, in the auditorium of the exhibition of the reconstruction of Spain, on July 3, 1940]. Madrid: Dirección General de Regiones Devastadas y Reparaciones, 1940.

Cárdenas Rodríguez, Gonzalo. "La Reconstrucción de Guernica." *Boletín de la Real Sociedad Vascongada de Amigos del País* 2, no. 2 (1946): 151–172.

Carey, John, ed. *Eyewitness to History*. Cambridge, Mass.: Harvard University Press, Cambridge, 1987.

Castresana, Luis. *El otro árbol de Guernica*. Bilbao: Caja de Ahorros Vizcaína, 1968.

Cava Mesa, María Jesús, María Silvestre, and Javier Arranz. *Memoria colectiva del bombardeo de Gernika* Gernika-Lumo: Gernika Gogoratuz, 1996.

Comité International du Coordination et d'Information pour l'Aide à l'Espagne Republicaine. *Guernica. La mainmise hitlérienne sur le Pays basque*, 1937.

Comité Mondial contre la Guerre et le Fascisme. *Bombardements et agressions en Espagne*. Paris, 1938.

Congressional Record. Proceedings and debates of the First Session of the First Session of the 75th Congress of the USA. Volume 81, Part 4, April 19, 1937, to May 18, 1937. Washington D.C.: United States Government Printing Office, 1937.

Corman, Mathieu. *¡Salud camarada! Cinq mois sur les fronts d'Espagne*. Paris: Editions Tribord, 1937.

Corum, James S. *Wolfram von Richthofen: Master of the German Air War*. Lawrence: University Press of Kansas, 2008.

Crozier, Brian. "Hoary Republican Myths." *National Review*, August 31, 1973, 938.

Crozier, Brian. *Franco, a Biographical History*. London: Eyre & Spottiswoode Ltd., 1967.

De la Cierva, Ricardo. *Historia actualizada de la Segunda República y la Guerra de España (1931–1939) con la denuncia de las patrañas.* Madrid: Fénix, 2003.

De La Cierva, Ricardo. "Guernica: Los documentos contra el mito." *Nueva y definitiva historia de la guerra civil*. Madrid: DINPE, 1986.

De La Cierva, Ricardo. "La polémica y la verdad sobre Guernica." In *España 1930–1977. La historia se confiesa*, 3 vols. Barcelona: Planeta, Barcelona, 1978. 3: 281–299.

Del Burgo, Jaime. *Conspiración y Guerra Civil*. Madrid: Alfaguara, 1970.

Durango, Ville martyre. Ce que furent les bombardements de la ville de Durango par les avions allemands. Comité Franco-espagnol, 1937.

Efecto de los bombardeos sobre ciudades españolas (frente de Vizcaya). May 28, 1937.

El clero vasco, fiel al Gobierno de la República, se dirige al Sumo Pontífice, para hacer constar que la vandálica destrucción de Durango y Guernica se debió exclusivamente a la acción de los aviones alemanes. Madrid and Valencia: Ediciones Españolas, May 11, 1937.

Elosegi, Joseba. *Quiero morir por algo*. Barcelona: Plaza and Janés, 1977.

Elosegi, Joseba and Ángel Viñas. "La destrucción de Guernica." *Historia 16*, no. 5 (September 1976): 131–137.

Foreign Wings over the Basque Country, The Friends of Spain, London, 1937.

Foreign Relations of the United States, Diplomat Papers, 1937, Vol. 1, General. Washington, D.C.: United States Printing Office, 1954.

Galland, Adolf. *Memorias. Los primeros y los últimos.* Barcelona: Editorial EHR, 1955.

Gamboa, José María and Jean-Claude Larronde, eds. *La guerra civil en Euzkadi: 136 testimonios inéditos recogidos por José Miguel de Barandiaran.* Milafranga: Bidasoa, 2005.

Garraghan, Gilbert J. *A Guide to Historical Method.* New York: Fordham University Press, 1946.

Gomá, Isidro. *Pastorales de la guerra de España.* Madrid: Ediciones Rialp, 1955.

Gomá, Isidro. *Respuesta obligada del cardenal arzobispo de Toledo Isidro Gomá Tomás.* Iruñea: s.n., 1937.

Guernica. Being the Official Report of a Commission Appointed by the National Government to Investigate the Causes of the Destruction of Guernica on April 26–28, 1937. London: Eyre & Spottiswoode Ltd., 1938.

Guernica. To civilized mankind. [Bilbao:] [Gobierno de Euskadi], 1937.

Guernica. Bilbao: Gobierno de Euzkadi, 1937.

Guernica. 26 de abril de 1937. Sólo el árbol vasco quedó en pie. Caracas, 1958.

Guernica. An Unimpeachable Testimony about the Crimes Committed by Fascism in Guernica. 1937.

Guernica. Being the Official Report of a Commission Appointed by the National Government to Investigate the Causes of the Destruction of Guernica on April 26–28, 1937. London: Eyre & Spottiswoode Ltd., 1938.

Guernica. El terrible 26 de abril de 1937. Caracas, 1958.

Guernica. The biography of a twentieth-century icon. New York: Bloomsbury, 2004.

Hart, Jeffrey. "The Great Guernica Fraud." *National Review*, January 5, 1973.

Herbert R. Southworth, vida y obra = Herbert R. Southworth, bizitza eta lana. Gernika-Lumo: Gernika-Lumoko Udala/Gernikako Bake Museoa, 2001.

Hitler, Adolf. *Hitler's Table Talk, 1941–1944: His Private Conversations.* New York: Enigma Books, 1951.

House of Commons. *Parliamentary Debates*, 5th series, volume 323, Official Report, in the second session of the 37th parliament of the United Kingdom of Great Britain and Northern Ireland, 7th volume of Session 1936–1937. London: His Majesty's Stationery Office, 1937.

House of Lords. *Parliamentary Debates*, 5th series, vol. 115. Official Report, in the second session of the 37th parliament of the United Kingdom of Great Britain and Northern Ireland, 2nd volume of Session 1936–1937. London: His Majesty's Stationery Office, 1937.

Howell, Martha C. and Walter Prevenier. *From Reliable Sources: An Introduction to Historical Methods.* Ithaca: Cornell University Press, 2001.

Informe sobre la situación de las Provincias Vascongadas bajo el dominio rojo-separatista. Valladolid: Universidad de Valladolid, 1938.

Irujo, Xabier. *El Gernika de Richthofen. Un ensayo de bombardeo de terror.* Gernika: Gernikako Bakearen Museoa Fundazioa/Gernika-Lumoko Udala, 2012.

Irujo, Xabier. *Gernika, 26 de abril de 1937.* Barcelona: Crítica, 2017.

Iturria, Joxe. *Memorias de Guerra.* Gernika: Gernika-Lumoko Udala, 2013.

Jaenecke, Erwin et al., *The German Luftwaffe in the Spanish Civil War.* Buxton: Military Library Research Service Ltd., 2006.

Jimenez de Aberasturi, Luis M. and Juan C. Jimenez de Aberasturi. *La guerra en Euskadi*. Donostia: Txertoa, 2007.

Jones, Adam. *Genocide: A Comprehensive Introduction*. New York: Routledge, 2011.

La destruction de Guernica. Paris: Comité Franco-espagnol, 1937.

Leguineche, Manuel. *Guernica, un horror experimental*. Los Grandes Hechos del Siglo XX, no. 1. Barcelona: Orbis, 1985.

Lopategui, José Ignacio. *Aita Patxi. Testimonio. 1ª parte: En la guerra (1937–1939)*. Bilbao: PP. Pasionistas, 1978.

Maier, Klaus A. *Guernica. La intervención alemana en España y el "caso Guernica."* Madrid: Sedmay, 1976.

Medlicott, W. N. and Douglas Dakin, eds. *Documents on British Foreign Policy (1919–1939)*. London: Her Majesty's Stationery Office, 1980.

Monks, Noel. *Eyewitness*. London: Frederick Muller Ltd., 1955.

Müller, Rolf-Dieter. *La muerte caída del cielo. Historia de los bombardeos durante la Segunda Guerra Mundial*. Barcelona: Destino, 2008.

Murua, Imanol. "Iñaki Murua. Gerra zibileko oroitzapenez elkarrizketa." Unpublished manuscript, 2009.

Neitzel, Sönke and Harald Welzer, eds. *Soldados del Tercer Reich: testimonios de lucha, muerte y crimen*. Barcelona: Crítica, 2012.

Neitzel, Sönke and Harald Welzer, eds. *Soldaten: On Fighting, Killing, and Dying: The Secret World War II Transcripts of German POWs*. Minneapolis: Highbridge, 2012.

Niebel, Ingo and Juantxo Egaña. *Gernika. Memoria de un pueblo bajo las bombas y el fuego*. Bilbao: Baigorri Argitaletxea, 2012.

Onaindia, Alberto. *Capítulos de mi vida I. Hombre de paz en la guerra*. Buenos Aires: Ekin, 1973.

Onaindia, Alberto. *Hombre de paz en la guerra*. Buenos Aires: Ekin, 1973.

Onaindia, Santiago. *Gernika*. Self-pub., 1987.

Pedriali, Ferdinando. *Guerra di Spagna e Aviazione Italiana*. Pinerolo: Società Storica Pinerolese, 1989.

Preston, Paul. *Franco: A Biography*. New York: Basic Books/HarperCollins, 1994.

Preston, Paul and Ann L. Mackenzie, eds. *The Republic Besieged: Civil War in Spain 1936–1939*. Edinburgh: Edinburgh University Press, 1996.

Raguer, Hilari. *Aita Patxi. Prisionero con los gudaris*. Barcelona: Claret, 2006.

Rankin, Nicholas. *Crónica desde Guernica. George Steer, corresponsal de guerra*. Madrid: Siglo XXI, 2005.

Rankin, Nicholas. *Telegram from Guernica: The Extraordinary Life of George Steer, War Correspondent*. London: Faber & Faber, 2003.

Ribbentrop, Joachim von. *The Ribbentrop Memoirs*. London: Weidenfeld and Nicolson, 1953.

Ricci, Corrado. *Vita di Pilota*. Milan: Mursia, 1976. 61–65.

Salas, Jesús. *Guernica, el bombardeo. La historia frente al mito*. Valladolid: Galland Books, 2012.

Salas, Jesús. *Guernica*. Madrid: Rialp, 1987.

Salas, Jesús. *Guernica: el bombardeo*. Madrid: Industrias Gráficas España, 1981.

Salas, Jesús. *Air War over Spain*. London: Ian Allan Ltd., 1974.

Salas, Jesús. "Guernica: la versión definitiva." *Nueva Historia* 1, no. 4 (May 1977): 27–50.

Shafer, Robert J., ed. *A Guide to Historical Method*. Chicago: Dorsey Press, 1980.

Schüler-Springorum, Stefanie. "El mito de Guernica: proyección, propaganda, política." *Historia del presente* 14, no. 2 (Nov. 2009): 123–136.

Smallwood, William. *The Day Guernica Was Bombed: A Story Told by Witnesses and Survivors*. Gernika: Gernikako Bakearen Museoko Fundazioa / Gernika-Lumoko Udala, 2012.

Smallwood, William. *El día en que Gernika fue bombardeada*. Gernika: Gernikako Bakearen Museoko Fundazioa / Gernika-Lumoko Udala, 2013.

Southworth, Herbert R. *La destrucción de Guernica: periodismo, diplomacia, propaganda e historia*. Granada: Comares, 2013.

Southworth, Herbert R. *Guernica! Guernica! A study of Journalism, Diplomacy, Propaganda and History*. Berkeley: University of California Press, 1977.

Southworth, Herbert R. *La destrucción de Guernica: periodismo, diplomacia, propaganda e historia*. Paris: Ruedo Ibérico, 1977.

Steer, George L. *The Tree of Gernika: A Field Study of Modern War*. London: Faber Finds, 2009.

Steer, George L. *The Tree of Gernika: A Field Study of Modern War*. London: Hodder and Stoughton, 1938.

Talón, Vicente. *Arde Guernica*. Madrid: San Martín, 1970.

Talón, Vicente. *El holocausto de Guernica*. Barcelona: Plaza & Janés, 1987.

Tarragó, Jean (Victor Montserrat). *Le drame d'un peuple incompris. La guerre au Pays Basque*. Paris: H. G. Peyre, 1937.

The Crime of Guernica. New York: Spanish Information Bureau, 1937.

Thomas, Gordon and Max Morgan-Witts. *Guernica. The Crucible of World War II*. New York: Ballantine Books, 1975.

Thomas, Hugh. "Heinkels over Guernica." *The Times Literary Supplement*, April 11, 1975.

United States Department of State, *Documents on German Foreign Policy* (1918–1945), Series D (1937–1945), Volume III, Germany and the Spanish Civil War (1936–1939). Washington, D.C.: United States Government Printing Office, 1950.

Unzueta, Humberto. "Las víctimas del bombardeo. La documentación básica." *Aldaba Gernika-Lumoko Aldizkaria* 86 (March–April 1997): 42–50.

Uriarte, Castor. *Bombas y mentiras sobre Guernica: acusa su arquitecto municipal cuando la guerra.* Bilbao: Gráficas Ellacuria, 1976.

Villa, Imanol. *Gernika, el bombardeo.* Bilbao: Idem4 & Expressive S.L., 2008.

Viñas, Ángel. "El bombardeo de Guernica. Aún faltan datos." *Historia 16,* No. 5, September 1976, pp. 135–137.

Viñas, Ángel. "Guernica, Quién lo hizo?" *Historia General de la Guerra Civil en Euskadi.* Bilbao: Naroki S.A. & Luis Haranburu, 1979. 165–215.

Viñas, Ángel. "Guernica. ¿El último fraude?" *Historia 16,* no. 9 (January 1977): 135–140.

Index

About the Author

Xabier Irujo is the chair of the Center for Basque Studies at the University of Nevada, Reno, where he is professor of genocide studies and the mentor of several graduate students. He was the first guest research scholar of the Manuel Irujo Chair at the University of Liverpool and has taught seminars on genocide and cultural genocide at Boise State University and at the University of California, Santa Barbara. He holds three master's degrees in linguistics, history and philosophy and has two PhDs in history and philosophy. Specialized in genocide studies, researching periods of Basque history related to both physical and cultural extermination, Dr. Irujo has lectured in various American and European universities and published on issues related to Basque history and politics. Member of the editorial board of four academic presses, Dr. Irujo has authored more than fifteen books and a number of articles in specialized journals and has received awards and distinctions at national and international level. His five books on the Gernika case are the result of more than twenty years of archival research that have brought to light thousands of unknown, unpublished documents, which are currently catalogued at the Documentation Center for the Bombing of Gernika. Dr. Irujo's research in this field has expanded our knowledge about this relevant topic in the history of terror bombing. His recent books include *Gernika 1937: The Market Day Massacre* (University of Nevada Press, 2015) and *The Bombing of Gernika* (Center for Basque Studies Press, 2018).

A summary of Prof. Irujo's CV is located at:
http://basque.unr.edu/academics-people-irujo.html